F is for Fiction

a nonfiction memoir

Emily W. Skinner

All Rights Reserved.
Original Manuscript Copyright 2024 by Emily W. Skinner
Published Copyright 2025 Emily W. Skinner

No part of this book may be reproduced or transmitted in any form or by any means, graphic, electronic, digital, or mechanical, including photocopying, recording, taping, or by any information storage retrieval system, without the permission in writing from the author.

ISBN: 978-1-7361911-6-3 paperback
ISBN: 978-1-7361911-7-0 hardback

This memoir includes remembrances written
in the context of the event and time.
Any terms, language, or phrases considered
offensive are unintentional.

Styled by *The Everything Grammar and Style Book*.
Reprinted stories follow original publisher's guidelines.

Book Cover Design by: www.Labelschmiede.com
Editor: Gretchen Wells
Book Formatter: Lisa DeSpain
www.book2bestseller.com

Other Books by Emily W. Skinner

Fiction by Emily W. Skinner

Hybrid Medical Thriller/Southern Noir
Mind Hostage

Romantic Suspense
Marquel (Book 1)
Marquel's Dilemma (Book 2)
Marquel's Redemption (Book 3)

Marquel Booktrailer:
Marquel book trailer on YouTube—
featuring actor Eric Roberts & Marquel Skinner
www.youtube.com/watch?v=6e6O7iYqeVQ

Coming of Age Humor
The Movie Queen

Young Adult Novels by E.W. Skinner
St. Blair: Children of the Night (Book 1)
Sybille's Reign (Book 2)
The Diary of St. Blair (Book 3)

Nonfiction by Emily W. Skinner
F Is for Fiction
A nonfiction memoir

Until We Sleep Our Last Sleep:
My Quaker Grandmother's Diary of Faith and
Community Amid Depression and Disability

The Diarist: A companion book for your inspired thoughts

For Me

It was nice getting reacquainted.

PART ONE

Becoming a writer

Featuring

Vincent Price
Milton Berle and Henny Youngman
Anthony Quinn
Margaret Papandreou
William Windom
Hank Williams, Jr.
Lillian Gish
The Murderer
Sam Shere
Bono
Paul McCartney
Cesar Romero
Patrick Wayne
Gary Burghoff
Jay Leno
Bohemian Chronicle
Marquel Booktrailer – Eric Roberts
Masterclass.com = Aaron Sorkin
Dough Nuts And More
Author Haunts

PART TWO

Harry Whittington

I Need To Let Harry Go

Master of the Roman Noir

The Lost Interview
Tucked Away In Indian Rocks …
A Writer With Many Names

Plotting Like Harry

PART ONE

Becoming a writer

F is for Fiction

Photo by Emily W Skinner

How do you get an F in Fiction? It's fiction. There are no rules, right? Other than not writing about real people and true events. That would be nonfiction.

Fiction was not a writing class.

Fiction should have been an easy A, had I studied my teacher's answer key. Somehow, I took the key as a guide to dive deeper into the meaning of symbolism, structure, and characterization versus just memorize the actual answers. I failed the class.

F'ed it.

As you can see from my report card, he went so far as to provide comment codes.

3. Study Habits Need Improving.

7. Student Appears to be Working Below Capacity.

My study habits weren't bad. I was working at capacity for my understanding. Where was my *ABC Afterschool Special?* "Emily Doesn't Know How to Learn."

To be totally transparent, I was an average to below average student in most everything. This report card shows Work Experience three times. The 9th period listing was classroom time. The 11th and 12th periods I left school to work. I'm guessing my employers provided feedback for those grades. I never asked. Work Experience was a dropout prevention program. How they determined my drop out potential—I'll never know? Was Work Experience perhaps foreshadowing? A term I should have grasped in Fiction.

Regarding my grades, before my parents' divorce, we moved a lot. We were members of the Retail Industrial Complex (not real). Our mission: aid consumers in buying affordable stuff on the department store level and thus keep American manufacturers manufacturing, distributors distributing, and homemakers homemaking. My father, a southern regional credit manager for the competition to McCroy, K-Mart and Zayre from about 1956 to 1970, was tasked with extending store credit to shoppers as the company's initiative to move more products, increase sales, and possibly put their competition out of business. Our retail family members were the employees of W.T. Grant Company. Cousins we'd never known. Dad, a company man, earned larger territory as he improved his stores' creditworthiness. W.T. Grant Company/Grants, like its rivals, slashed prices and kept their margins super low to capture more market share hoping that volume sales would balance any potential risk. We were a corporate American casualty.

A family toppled when our captain was stripped of his rank on our final family troop movement to Florida in 1969. The Brandon store, the final battle, a city with no retail adversary was a gold mine. But it didn't last long. The chain closed nationwide in 1976 by putting itself out of business through an extension of credit to *all* (starting in 1969).

In my father's defense, God rest his soul, I know he wouldn't have agreed to such a risky proposition, as my mother is living proof. My Dad ran my mother's and grandmother's credit when they got engaged. It could have ended my future existence, as Mom considered breaking the engagement. Dad, on the other hand, wasn't going to marry into bad credit and Mom wasn't going to be reduced to a credit score. Thankfully, they patched up my grandmother's credit, got married and produced four children. Oddly, Dad spent his dying days in a nursing facility a few blocks from the former Brandon store. Fortunately, he had another career of greater importance with a greater legacy, but Grants was always his first love, then Mom, his children and eventually his second wife.

Today, Brandon, Florida looks as though retail contagion spread over every square mile (33.14* square miles). There is not a parcel of available commercial land left in my estimation. Not so in the late sixties. Clayton Plaza was a new shopping center and W.T. Grant and Publix grocer were anchors among small mom and pop stores. Otherwise, you would have to travel to Tampa if Grants didn't have it. *Size determined by Census.gov.

With each relocation, my knowledge decreased. It seemed there were no overlapping courses of study from one state to another. Or perhaps there was, and it was the way it was taught that eluded me? I am a left-handed right-brain thinker, a complication all by itself. Which brings me to Logic. I did poorly in Logic, too. It felt like science, but it was math. Right? The fact that I don't know for sure says a lot. I Googled it. Search results included topics ranging from *Is Logic an English or Math class?* To, *We have* (Logic) *courses in the Sciences and the various branches of Mathematics.* Glad it's not just me. The first week I got into the Logic pattern of thinking, then lost it over a weekend. I might have fared better mastering a Rubix's Cube for a grade. Not really. But a good challenge for me would be baking a scratch cake or rolling dough that doesn't cling to me and transfers to everything I touch.—I still have a life goal to make rice pudding that doesn't turn into a rice cake, things like that. Home Economics was never available at any school I transferred to. Instead, I got redirected to Choral and Music Appreciation. I'm an alto. Altos sang the background vocals, "Parsley, sage, rosemary and thyme," in our classes' practice run of Simon and Garfunkel's *Scarborough Fair*. I won't mention more since I'm not knowledgeable of music royalties and wouldn't want to deplete my historically meager book earnings any further. Anyhow, my homemaking skills are subpar, having never been taught to properly cook an egg for a grade, read a recipe, sew a hem or whatever else the Department of Education required for graduation.

My parents, as a married couple, were all about education. They wanted successful offspring. Divorce changed that. Dropout prevention didn't work. I quit day school or *real school* as my teachers called it, at sixteen to work full-time. I didn't need proms and things my peers enjoyed, I only wanted the diploma. Thus, I enrolled myself in my high school's night school where I finished on time. We night-schoolers arrived after our day jobs to buckle down and get our credits. There was no such thing as Home Economics in night school. We learned Americanism vs. Communism and worldly stuff like that, along with whatever English, Math and History earned the certificate. And, having never lucked into my course preferences at any school I attended, I enrolled in, and completed driver's education at our local Safer Dixie Driving School with my own money. I also bought a brown metallic Plymouth Valiant. My employer co-signed the car loan.

So, I am writing nonfiction. It's all true. Sounds very Coen Brothers, but mine is true. Not as dramatic as *Fargo*, but there was a murder. I'm sandwiching in celebrity interviews and articles I wrote for newspapers to prove I did try to make a go of journalism. As a twentysomething I had a goal to earn a degree in mass communications and write stories that mattered. Not that the stories you are about to read matter, but hopefully they'll entertain. Most were previously published. At one point I thought I wanted to be the next Ann Rule, who wrote about Ted Bundy and other criminals. I was fascinated by Truman Capote's *In Cold Blood*, too. However, it turns out I don't like killers, I feel for victims. Those left behind. The Murderer chapter is my only endeavor at writing true crime. I didn't know the victims, but I was acquainted with one of the murderers.

So, as with most things I start, I took a shortcut from college to cub reporter. I completed all the electives for mass communications at St. Petersburg Jr. College, not a degree and then sold a newspaper editor on my eagerness to be their woman on the street and got hired. Editors like enthusiasm. Most people do. As such, I've been asked more times than I care to recall to—*calm down, slow down, settle down, give it a rest,* or *sleep on it*. I'm loud. I speak over people, shout questions, and attempt to dominate a discussion. It comes instinctively. I also have hearing loss, so the loud thing seems a natural compensation for needing audible voices. Hence, I become the most noticeable voice, unknowingly. Well, until someone says to *keep it down*.

To be clear, I didn't last long in the investigative reporting field because I was never an investigative reporter. I got ahead of myself at times. Before I knew it, I was sitting with the First Lady of

Greece, or in a limo with Hank Williams, Jr. wishing I could snap my fingers and disappear. As a feature writer, sometimes city council reporter, previewer of entertainment, and theater critic (who had no right to criticize—long before it became a social media norm), I was able to acquire assignments by just asking for the opportunity. The stories I pursued as a stringer (freelancer) for local newspapers didn't always find a home. I include some here. Most of my theater critiques I shredded as penance for any harm I may have caused a budding actor. I am not saying their performance was better than my criticism. Well, I'm also not saying that my criticism was Pulitzer Prize winning either. Like shouldn't my editor have said, "That's a bit harsh for a little theatre performance." Or "Aren't they running a big ad in the weekend edition? Shouldn't you tone it down, so they can sell enough seats to pay for the ad?" Things I was too naïve to consider. Not that a writer should sell out because an advertiser supports the paper but rather have some understanding of community-based organizations and a little compassion. But in all fairness, I did pan Richard Harris in *Camelot* as it felt he just didn't make an effort, just walked through the St. Petersburg performance. I loved Richard Harris in the day, but didn't favor him as a result.

To all actors I know, including those in my family, remember a writer's performance is on the page (we get bad reviews, too). We don't have to remember lines, hit a mark, or audition to get the story. Actors, please accept ticket sales, applause, and peer approval, as the true measure of your work, not a critic's opinion (unless it's a rave review!). But seriously, Anthony Quinn (see my article) stressed that an actor needs thick skin to put up with the slights and humiliations of the profession, which I think is an important thread in this book. Many of us find ourselves following or ignoring our instincts or the counsel of others and sometimes succeeding, oftentimes failing at varied life experiences. Thus, these essays and articles are about how it feels to labor at the dream. How the people we look up to are often as insecure, hurt or as doubtful as we are and don't necessarily see their own success the way we do.

I digress.

Back to the newspapers—I got hired as a staff writer at the weekly paper and laid off after maybe a year? Come to think of it, I'm not sure if I was laid off-laid off or *laid off*. Meaning, was this a gentle way to get rid of me because I wasn't performing to their expectations, or was it a big layoff? My bosses stayed at the weekly division. I (didn't know better) had the audacity to approach the parent company for work. I had bills to pay. One of the daily editors listened to my layoff woes, treated me like a peer, and gave me assignments. Talk about luck. My byline moved up. Weeklies were a rung down from the daily newspaper. I became a stringer for the daily! The daily! I moved up. Perhaps the assignment editor gave me stories to chase me out of the newsroom? No complaints here. Then a cinematic moment happened. The publisher gathered everyone available to a spot just outside his office. This was real. He waved a particular section of the paper and shouted, "Who is this woman? Why am I paying a stringer to write everything when I have staff writers?!"

I was noticed!

Anyway, what brought him to the boiling point was a misspelling. I meant cavalry and spelled calvary. He went on, "Does anyone know how to spell? Calvary is the hill where Christ died!" Or some heated variation of the same sentiment. Everyone looked around. I did, too. *Sloppy writer!* No need to introduce myself now. Afterall, we all entered and exited the same back entrance never looking up to say hello or goodbye. I kept my mouth shut. This was also my editor's typo. After the scolding, everyone went back to their desk and the clickity-clack of typing. I got fewer assignments.

I also married, eventually had kids and worked for investment bankers as my newspaper gig dried up. My husband (Tom) and I even tried entrepreneurship. We became a statistical average. It sounds like a good thing. Statistical average! But not so. We owned a small business that failed in the first year. Our second business lasted three years. Then I moved into sales. My first attempt at sales was before I married at the encouragement of a real estate broker who saw the gift of gab in me. He suggested I try selling real estate. My mother thought it was a great idea. So, I took the real estate course and the Florida Real Estate License exam and finished question 100 in the number 99 answer block. F'ed it. And remarkably, I made a shortcut into real estate, too. My mother found a little house with an unfinished detached studio/garage in a newspaper ad. She figured this was my chance to get started as a real estate mogul (her dream). Anyway, the little house was owned by world renown *Life Magazine* photographer, Sam Shere. Shere was best known for the Hindenburg explosion photos in *Life*. I didn't know who Shere was at the time. My down payment was small. He held the mortgage. And we developed a three-year relationship through his recurrent foreclosure threats. Refer to the Sam Shere chapter.

Along the way I dipped my toe back into the writing pond to publish others (see Bohemian Chronicle), write novels (see Harry Whittington) and screenplays (see Dough Nuts and More) all while working a day job. So, without further ado and in no particular order we'll stumble into my past.

Since I have confessed to villainy as a critic of theater performers, it seems appropriate to start with Vincent Price. He understood better than most that villains don't start out as such.

Clearwater Sun
SUNDAY, January 26, 1986
SECTION D

THE VILLAIN

It's the price Vincent pays for playing so many

By EMILY SKINNER
Sun correspondent

When one thinks of him, they think villain. And villains are exactly what Vincent Price will talk about Tuesday evening at Ruth Eckerd Hall.

"The Villain Still Pursues Me" is just one of many topics the famed "horror" star lectures on. In a telephone interview from his home in Los Angeles, Price talked about villains and villainy, as well as his other pet projects.

"Villains have served a classic function in films. I discuss them in a light way," Price said. "The villain never sets out to be a villain; rather he seeks revenge. The villain is the person you least expect and the one who keeps the plot going.

"I've played so many that I can now watch a show or movie and usually pick them out 90 percent of the time," the 74-year-old actor said.

Is today's villain too closely associated with today's criminal?

"Oh yes," Price said emphatically. "The classic villain is not a criminal. They're evil in spite of themselves. That's what makes (Charles) Manson so fascinating. He said.

Photo by Emily W Skinner

He also feels that films like "Halloween," "Friday the 13th and "Dawn Of the Dead" are too permissive. "They don't have far to go when they kill everyone off in the first 15 minutes. There is no suspense, no comedy relief. In a good thriller, the villain is never revealed until the end.

"There have been lots of spoofs of the old-fashioned horror films, melodramas. And, I think we may come back around to that," he said.

One mini-spoof that Price narrated was Michael Jackson's hit "Thriller."

"I think I was selected for that, because there was no one else alive to do it (meaning a Boris Karloff or the like)," he joked.

A native of St. Louis, Mo., Price graduated from Yale University with a Bachelor of Arts degree and later attended the University of London. His first appearance on the stage was in London's Gate Theater.

He was later discovered by producer Gilbert Miller, who cast the 23-year-old Price opposite Helen Hayes in the Broadway premiere of "Victoria Regina."

His credits include Orson Welles' Mercury Theater productions and 100-plus films. Most memorable of his many films are "The House Of Wax," "The House of Seven Gables," "The Song of Bernadette," "Laura," "The Three Musketeers," "The Raven," "The Pit and the Pendulum," "The Abominable Dr. Phibes" and his favorite, "The Theater of Blood."

His co-star in the "Theater of Blood," Coral Browne, he later married. The two can now be seen on commercials for Citibank.

"The Theater of Blood' is my favorite because I met my wife doing it. It is a basic revenge play. It had a good cast and I loved doing it," Price elaborated.

> "The classic villain is not a criminal. They're evil in spite of themselves. That's what makes (Charles) Manson so fascinating."
>
> He said.

When talking about the many horror films he has made, he talks with a certain affinity of Boris Karloff, Basil Rathbone and Peter Lorrie.

"They were gentle people and fun. We were not doing Shakespeare. But, we enjoyed what we were doing. They were not violent (films). They were good pictures, innocent," Price said.

His other passions include art and cooking. He hosted a TV program, "Cooking Price-Wise," which included gourmet recipes and his favorite delicacies.

"I cook at home now. They (producers) want you to cook seven-course meals. I'm not up to that," Price said laughingly.

In the world of art, Price lectures on such subjects as "Modern Art," "Primitive Art," "The Letters of Van Gogh" and "The Enjoyment of Great Art."

He is the past chairman of the Indian Arts and Crafts Board for the U.S. Department of the Interior, a member of the Royal Society of Arts and the Arts Council of UCLA. He also has been a member of the Fine Arts Committee for the White House, as well as a member of the Board of Trustees of Scripps College and the Los Angeles County Museum of Art.

He would most like to be remembered, he said, as a guy who enjoyed his career, life and art, and was well-known because someone let him in.

Vincent Price will present "The Villains Still Pursue Me" at 8 p.m. Tuesday at Ruth Eckerd Hall,

1111 McMullen-Booth Road. Tickets are S13.50.

F IS FOR FICTION

Laughs
Milton Berle, Henny Youngman find opposites distract

By EMILY W. SKINNER

"Take Milton and Henny," the title of a cable special Milton Berle and Henny Youngman have been putting together, is just one of many projects these two show business giants have been working on. Saturday, Jan. 11, the comic duo will give two performances at Clearwater's Ruth Eckerd Hall.

In separate phone interviews, Youngman's from his home in New York and Berle's from the Friars Club in California, they discussed their current activities, as well as some memories from the past.

"Berle and myself have been heckling each other for 50 years. We've been wanting to put a show together. We did and it was a bonanza," said the noted "king of the one liners." "Since we're both booked with the William Morris Agency, we began to book more dates and we call the show 'A Night of a Thousand Laughs.' It's like a big house party.

"You know Berle was sick recently," Youngman said. "He had a charisma bypass (referring to Berle's quadruple bypass surgery last year)."

Milton Berle explained that he originated the idea of "A Thousand Laughs."

"Youngman and I have been friends for years," Berle said. "We are complete opposites. Our styles are completely different.

"'A Night of A Thousand Laughs,' if you want to count all of them, is not the same every show. We improvise here and there. We want everyone to have a good time," Berle said.

Both agree they are opposites. They travel to their shows separately, arriving at a schedule that suits them individually, and they maintain their own style. Berle seems to call most of the shots, while Youngman appears to be along for the ride.

Berle admits to being a perfectionist. But he feels that he is more involved with detail and getting the job done right, than being a perfectionist. It's a quality Youngman admires.

"I called the shots (on his television show)," Berle said. "You only get one shot at it. I was and still am a perfectionist.

MILTON BERLE
... a 'perfectionist'

That's true. I am a perfectionist."

Both men started out in vaudeville and climbed their own show business ladder to success. Youngman began as a fiddle player. He played dances and moved up to fiddle-playing joke teller and later appeared regularly on the "Kate Smith Show."

Berle began as a vaudevillian and later became known to millions as "Uncle Miltie" on his own show, the "Texaco Star Theater" and later "The Milton Berle Show."

A veteran and pioneer of live television, Berle said that he did more than 3,000 shows between June 10, 1948, and 1954.

"You only had one chance; there was no second chance. You couldn't take it (a sketch) again," Berle said. "You make the most of it. Do a little ad-libbing. If a shoe fell off, you tried to recover it.

"We didn't have a laugh machine back then, like the ones you hear on sit-coms. I don't believe in that. If the joke died, the joke died," Berle said.

Back then, bloopers were live, Berle continued. He now feels that shows have to create bloopers to fill the blooper shows. He also said that the ability to re take a scene may make for a lazy performer.

The craziest blooper that happened on his show, Berle recalls, was an incident that involved comedian Red Buttons. Berle asked Buttons to take off his clothes. When Buttons

HENNY YOUNGMAN
... 'king of the one liners'

didn't do so, Berle was to grab a certain part of the suit and pull it off. Berle grabbed the collar of the suit instead and pulled everything off Buttons.

"He stood there nude. What every person saw, they saw," Berle said.

When Youngman isn't busy performing he likes to visit Manhattan's Carnegie Deli. "Lots of show business people go there. It's a nice place. They treat us right."

"I took G. David (Clearwater entertainer G. David Howard) there when he was up visiting," he said. "I played down there (at G. David's) early in the season. Then he came up here."

Does he think comedians today are as good as he and Milton were when they started? Said Youngman: "They are all right for five minutes, but they are not better than we were."

Berle, on the other hand, would not answer the question. He would only say that too many comedians today use four-letter words on behalf of themselves.

"A Night of a Thousand Laughs," starring Milton Berle with special guest "distraction" Henny Youngman, is slated for 5 and 9 p.m. Saturday, Jan. 11, at Ruth Eckerd Hall, 1111 McMullen-Booth Road. Tickets are $14.95, $13.95, $11.95 and $10.95. Tickets can be purchased at Maas Brothers and the Eckerd box office. For more information call 725-1844.

Photo by Emily W Skinner

Milton Berle Talked to My Grandmother

The brief words they exchanged were dramatic to me. My namesake grandmother Emily had agreed to watch her great-granddaughter, my daughter, so I could run to the Clearwater Sun Newspaper office to do a phone interview with Milton Berle. Now mind you, Milton and Grandma were roughly the same age. He was a comedy legend. My grandmother (a modest humored former Western Union employee who during World War II was sent from Charlotte, N.C. to Los Angeles, California to type communication and later retire from teletyping for Celanese Corporation) enjoyed work. So, when I asked her to babysit, she didn't bat an eye.

Facebook – Uncredited Public Domain photo

Interestingly enough, Milton Berle would not provide his home telephone number or call me from his home's landline. Not that I had any way of knowing an incoming number on a landline then—other than having police trace the call. Caller I.D. wouldn't be invented and rolled out to consumers until the early 1990s, so tracing a call required a warrant and to my knowledge not at a reporter's request. But seriously, I was challenged enough writing on my Commodore 64 home computer utilizing floppy disk technology. Pulling a disk out of the floppy drive before the light signaled it finished saving my story would render my file unretrievable (similar to a premature thumb drive release today), which happened a few times. I was no threat. If I had called him from my house, I would have had to pay long-distance calling fees which the newspaper didn't reimburse. Well, not stringers. And for those too young to remember, long distance was a call outside of your immediate area code, which was pretty much the world. As such, driving back and forth to the newspaper office was more affordable as gas was cheaper back then. Nevertheless, Berle wanted to keep his private information private. He had trust issues and agreed to call me at the Clearwater Sun office from The Friars Club of Beverly Hills, California also known as The Friars' Club of California, a west coast version of New York's Friars Club. Berle was a founding member of the California organization.

When I got to the Clearwater Sun office, ready to sit by the phone, an editor informed me he gave my home phone number to Milton Berle. The comedian would call me at home. Damn it! So, I left the newsroom, ran down the back stairs, got into my car and drove home very fast. As soon as I entered, my grandmother said, "Milton Berle would like for you to call him at The Friars Club."

No!

I stared at my grandmother. Stunned. You'd have thought she was *his* personal secretary. My first instinct was to question whether she'd written the phone number down correctly, but I quickly realized I was in the presence of a master. She didn't make mistakes. She was a Western Union ace.

What to do? I could drive back to the office and risk Berle leaving The Friars Club, perhaps believing I was inconsiderate having not been at the newspaper office hours earlier (than the appointed time) to receive his original call. Or I could spend the money on a long-distance call. Hmm. Do I call from our Florida Room aka enclosed porch? The temperatures got warm back there unless I turned on the wall air conditioning unit which was noisy. Should I sweat and talk? Is my comfort important?

I decided to call from my bedroom where the computer and printer sat perched on my grandmother's claw-footed dining table (my oversized desk) that needed refinishing but had the leaf removed and one side folded down (so you have a visual). The crowded bedroom also had a ceiling fan, a chair, a double bed, one bedside table, a chest of drawers and a dresser. This room got warm with the door closed as we didn't have central heat and air in our two-bedroom home. My young husband had determined there was no way professionals could install central heating and air conditioning in our house. A design flaw, he assured me and besides we couldn't afford it. We instead relied on a wall A.C. unit in our living room and Florida Room, fans in our bedrooms for sixteen years until the next owner immediately installed central heat and air—by magic I presume, since they weren't aware of the design flaw.

So, I called the Friars Club and Milton Berle answered immediately. Impressive! I heard a lot of background noise on his end. I imagined him sitting in a wooden enclosed phone booth with the door open, smoking a cigar like a boss and watching club happenings. I have no clue what the inside of the Friars Club looks like. Anyway, I asked questions and he answered. I was awestruck.

I also called Henny Youngman but from the newspaper office to avoid the long-distance cost. He was very sweet and friendly.

Berle strictly business. I don't remember much about the Youngman call. Since deadlines for daily papers are daily, the writing pressure was instantaneous. No room for procrastination. How do I write this? I weaved their interviews together since they were doing a joint event. I started by getting all the quotes down and then worked on adding any nuisances and of course, highlighting the event that was coming, then I'd reread all and work on making sense of it. If you look at the two images of the article, these are from the daily and weekly paper. Selling an article to the daily paper, a stringer was paid a flat rate for the article. It might also be distributed in the parent company's various editions and weekly papers, which was wonderful as far as reaching a wider audience, but it didn't earn me more money.

Meeting a deadline was a relief, as well as nausea inducing. An editor took over once I saved a story on the newspaper's system. *What did I turn in?* I'd question everything—but couldn't do anything about it. There was no printout. There wasn't a thumb drive to keep a copy. The only evidence I had was my notes. All I could do was wait till it printed. So, the next day I'm looking for it, expecting major edits and to be buried with multiple jumps around ill-fitting ads. These were the days of paste up.

Surprise!

I had the lead story for the entertainment section. Then I start reading my cobbled quotes, knowing I could have done better. But hey, what a clip for the portfolio!

Henny Youngman and Milton Berle
Opposites Distract

A Night of a THOUSAND LAUGHS

Clearwater Sun
WEDNESDAY, January 8, 1986
Sun Living SECTION C

By EMILY W. SKINNER
Sun correspondent

"Take Milton and Henny," the title of a cable special Milton Berle and Henny Young have been putting together, is just one of many projects these two show business giants have been working on. Saturday, Jan. 11, the comic duo will give two performances at Clearwater's Ruth Eckerd Hall.

In separate phone interviews, Youngman's from his home in New York and Berle's from the Friars Club in California, they discussed their current activities, as well as some memories from the past.

"Berle and myself have been heckling each other for 50 years. We've been wanting to put a show together. We did and it was a bonanza," said the noted "king of the one liners." "Since we're both booked with William Morris Agency, we began to book more dates and we call the show "A Night of a Thousand Laughs." It' s like a big house party.

"You know Berle was sick recently," Youngman said. "He had a charisma bypass (referring to Berle's quadruple bypass surgery last year)."

Milton Berle explained that he originated the idea of "A Thousand Laughs."

"Youngman and I have been friends for years," Berle said. "Our styles are completely different. A Night of A Thousand Laughs, if you want to count all of them, is not the same every show. We improvise here and there. We want everyone to have a good time," Berle said.

Both agree they are opposites. They travel to their shows separately, arriving at a schedule that suits them individually, and they maintain their own style. Berle seems to call most of the shots, while Youngman appears to be along for the ride.

Berle admits to being a perfectionist. But he feels that he is more involved with detail and getting the job done right, than being a perfectionist. It's a quality Youngman admires.

"I called the shots (on his television show)." Berle said. "You only get one shot at it. I was and still am a perfectionist."

Both men started out in vaudeville and climbed their own show business ladder to success. Youngman began as a fiddle player. He played dances and moved up to fiddle-playing joke teller and later appeared regularly on the "Kate Smith Show."

Berle began as a vaudevillian and later became known to millions as "Uncle Miltie" on his own show, the "Texaco Star Theater" and later "The Milton Berle Show."

A veteran and pioneer of live television, Berle said that he did more than 3,000 shows between June 10, 1948, and 1954.

"You only had one chance; there was no second chance. You couldn't take it (a sketch) again," Berle said. "You make the most of it. Do a little adlibbing. If a shoe fell off, you tried to recover it.

"We didn't have a laugh machine back them, like the ones you hear on sit-coms. I don't believe in that. If the joke died, the joke died," Berle said.

Back then, bloopers were live, Berle continued. He now feels that shows have to create bloopers to fill the blooper shows. He also said that the ability to re-take a scene may make for a lazy performer.

The craziest blooper that happened on his show, Berle recalls, was an incident that involved comedian Red Buttons.

Berle asked Buttons to take off his clothes. When Buttons didn't do so, Berle was to grab a certain part of the suit and pull it off. Berle grabbled the collar of the suit instead and pulled everything off of Buttons.

"He stood there nude. What every person saw, they saw," Berle said.

When Youngman isn't busy performing he likes to visit Manhattan's Carnegie Deli. "Lots of show business people go there. It's a nice place. They treat us right."

"I took G. David (Clearwater entertainer G. David Howard) there when he was up visiting," he said. "I played down there (at G. David's) early in the season. Then he came up here."

Does he think comedians today are as good as he and Milton when were when they started? Said Youngman: "They are all right for five minutes, but they are not better than we were."

Berle on the other hand, would not answer the question. He would only say that too many comedians today use four-letter words on behalf of themselves.

"A Night of a Thousand Laughs," starring Milton Berle with special guest "distraction" Henny Youngman, is slated for 5 and

"You know Berle was sick recently," Youngman said. "He had a charisma bypass (referring to Berle's quadruple bypass surgery last year)."

9 p.m. Saturday, Jan. 11, at Ruth Eckerd Hall, 1111 Mc-Mullen-Booth Road. Tickets are $14.95, $13.95, $11.95 and $10.95. Tickets can be purchased at Maas Brothers and the Eckerd box office. For more information call 725-1844.

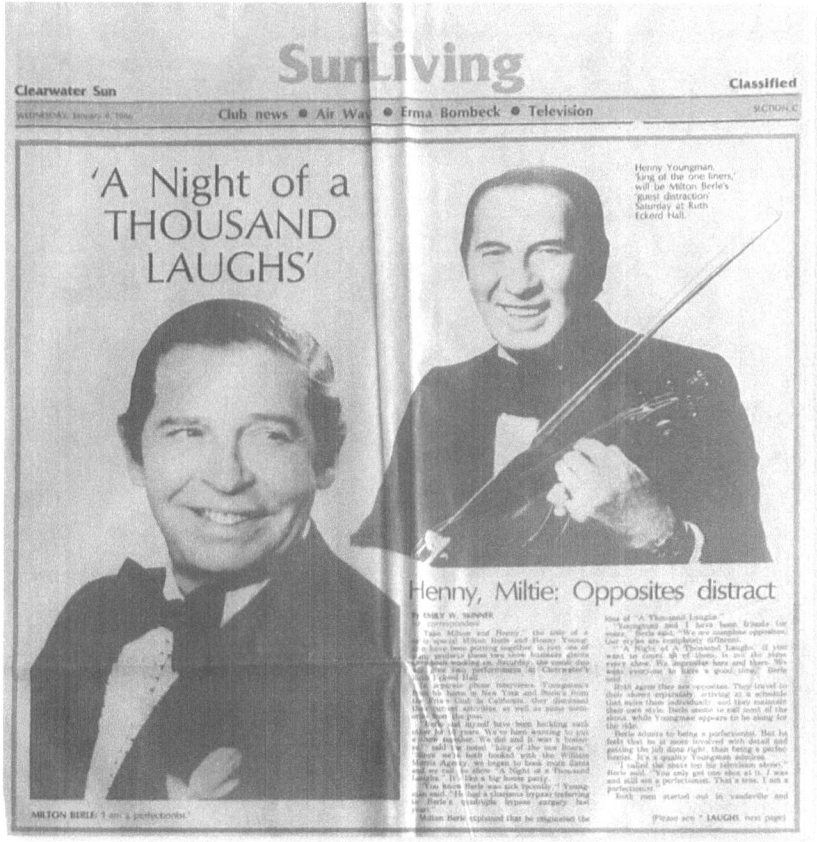

Photo by Emily W Skinner

Cover One, Get One Free!

Anthony Quinn and Margaret Papandreou

The Florida of my youth saw the largest loyal fanbase of movie stars from the Golden Era of Hollywood. These legends headlined our local dinner theaters, guest-lectured at colleges in addition to concert halls and many retired to our state. So, anytime a celebrity opportunity presented itself, I raised my hand, whether a preview, interview or review.

With notepad, camera and pocket change ready for pay phones –cellphones didn't exist, I arrived at Anthony Quinn's talk early. While writing in my reporter's notebook, a Greek television crew spotted and informed me Margaret Papandreou was speaking nearby. She was their next stop after Quinn. They said I should go with them to interview her, offering to take me directly to her. I thought about it. Of course I should. Papandreou sounded familiar, but I had no idea who she was. As the television crew spoke to each other in Greek and nodded at me, I didn't want to admit that Greek government—*was Greek to me*. Every now and then one crew member would come over and say, "You'll want to ask her…" Something political. I gave them a *we'll see* expression, which I think came off as an affirmative to them. Before Quinn came on, I used the college office's phone and let my editor know

I had another story and photos coming, unless someone else was covering Papandreou? No, go ahead, I was told. They didn't know she was in town. Thanks to the television guys, I looked smart—chasing a solid lead! Scooping the newsroom!

This required background information, stat. But I'd have to wait until I got back to the newspaper's morgue, a library of past news articles, to learn more about the First Lady of Greece. This was before Google and the internet. Often talent agents supplied public relations highlights and bios of their clients ahead of an event. A publicity packet might hint to interview questions or provide greater detail on the subject or individual. The morgue was my primary resource. The best I could hope for was an inter-office envelope of clippings or promotional materials to build a list of questions before a happening –or find what I could after the fact to fill article gaps with relevant information, which I needed in this situation.

I was to cover Anthony Quinn's appearance at SPJC and the Prime Minister of Greece's wife's visit to Tarpon Springs. I didn't have time to call my mother and quiz her for possible anecdotes. She knew something about everyone in the news it seemed. She was my phone-a-friend before *Who Wants To Be A Millionaire* was a show. So I decided to stick with the basics: Who, What, Where, When and Why.

Quinn stood tall and in close proximity to those in attendance. He was there for an art talk but sprinkled in his opinions about acting and living in American. I got the impression that he wanted to set the record straight that while he was born in Mexico and a U.S. resident, no one had better challenge his allegiances. In those early days, I wanted to avoid paraphrasing too much. I'd jot lots of quotes to capture the moment and often my quote ratio was off balance. I relied too heavily on quotes and didn't note enough about my surroundings or the tempo of the room. The Greek television folks grabbed the actor for a quick on camera Q&A afterward and motioned me to follow them. I did not approach Quinn. A missed opportunity for sure.

Funny enough, I received a phone call from a *Clearwater Sun* reader the following week. A staffer called me over and said a subscriber wanted to talk to me about the Anthony Quinn article. I thought *oh, crap, what did I do?* An older gentleman said he was reliving the moment in reading the article. He asked how I could remember it all. I thanked him for the compliment and reread the article. He was far too generous. Letters from locals I interviewed were occasional, but this was a first from a reader. I've never forgotten the call and the confidence it gave me.

When I got to Margaret Papandreou's Tarpon Springs stopover, I stood near the television guys. They'd given me talking points to throw at Papandreou. I had no clue what they were talking about and wouldn't repeat anything. If they weren't willing to ask these questions, why should I? When she finished her chat, they ushered me over and I introduced myself. Papandreou sat with me for a few minutes and then she was off to her next engagement. I sincerely wondered if I could write anything that made sense. See article below for the end result.

F IS FOR FICTION

* Actor Anthony Quinn speaks to SPJC crowd

(from page 1A)

"I used to go by this antique shop, and there was a clay horse," he said. "I don't know what it was; I just liked it."

Later the shop owner, who had noticed Quinn looking through the window often, invited him inside. Quinn said he thought the man feared he might try to steal the figure.

"I told him some day I would own it," Quinn said. "It was $150. You know he asked me how much money I had. I dug in my pockets, and I had 35 cents. He took it as a down payment, and I paid for it for seven years."

He added that he recently was offered $300,000 for the clay horse.

"There is a great misunderstanding about what art is all about," the actor-artist said. "You cannot define art—I'm sorry to say this—as you cannot define God."

But he added, "A true artist is a prophet."

He also said the American artist is too unrealistic. "American's have a watered-down version of the way life is," he said, making his point by giving examples of hit fantasy films such as "Star Wars" and "E.T."

"Americans have a tendency to not face reality," the outspoken Quinn contended.

When asked were he lives, Quinn said he had homes all over the world but remains a United States citizen: "I pay 70 percent of my income to American taxes. That way I have my right to protest. If I don't like something, then I can protest."

Clad in black trousers and a navy-blue pull-over shirt, Quinn also talked about his family and children, revealing that his 19-year-old son, Frank, had accompanied him on the trip. He later introduced his son to the audience.

"There are things that sons don't say to fathers and fathers don't say to sons," Quinn noted. "I'm glad that my son is here. Maybe he'll find out something he wanted to know."

He also said he did not want to raise his children in the United States, because of a "success syndrome" that he said is apparent in the American way of life.

> 'I went to acting school, and at 19, I was in a play. Well, every line I said, I got a laugh. I later found out it was because my fly was open. So I left my fly open and became an actor.'
>
> —Anthony Quinn

Anthony Quinn talks to a crowd of fans.

Actor Anthony Quinn talks art at SPJC

By EMILY L. WILLIAMS
Sun staff writer

TARPON SPRINGS—"You have to have skin as thick as a rhinoceros to be an actor . . . to go through those terrible indignities and rejection," international film star Anthony Quinn told a crowd of fans in St. Petersburg Junior College's lecture hall Friday.

Quinn was in Pinellas County as a special guest of the Pinellas County Arts Council, which held its black tie gala Friday evening at the Don Ce Sar Hotel in St. Petersburg.

"I would never want any of my children to go into acting" he said in his address at SPJC.

Quinn said he did not seek to be an actor early in his life. As a teen, he said, he won a contest that gave him a chance to study architecture with Frank Lloyd Wright.

Quinn said Wright asked what was wrong with his speech and suggested Quinn take acting lessons.

Quinn later admitted he had a speech disorder as a youth and underwent surgery and speech theraphy.

"I went to acting school, and at 19, I was in a play," he said. "Well, every line I said, I got a laugh. I later found out it was because my fly was open. So I left my fly open and became an actor."

But the two-time Oscar winner (for "Viva Zapata" in 1952 and "Lust for Life" in 1956) and veteran of more than 100 films said he has not decided whether he is an actor yet. Quinn said he still feels he is in a learning process.

"I want a new life, another crack at it," the 67-year-old Quinn said.

When it comes to art, Quinn does more than act. Quinn is a sculptor, writer, painter and an architect—he currently is building a village in Italy.

And he collects art as well. Quinn said he began that endeavor at the age of 19, when he was very poor.

(* Please see ACTOR, next page)

Photos by Emily W Skinner

November 6, 1982
Clearwater Sun

Actor Anthony Quinn talks art at SPJC

By EMILY L. WILLIAMS
Sun staff writer

TARPON SPRINGS – "You have to have skin as thick as rhinoceros to be an actor …to go through those terrible indignities and rejection," international film star Anthony Quinn told a crowd of fans in St. Petersburg Junior College's lecture hall Friday.

Quinn was in Pinellas County as a special guest of the Pinellas County Arts Council, which held its black-tie gala Friday evening at the Don CeSar Hotel in St. Petersburg.

"I would never want any of my children to go into acting" he said in his address at SPJC.

Quinn said he did not seek to be an actor early in his life. As a teen, he said, he entered a contest that gave him a chance to study architecture with Frank Lloyd Wright.

Quinn said Wright asked what was wrong with his speech and suggested Quinn take acting lessons.

Quinn later admitted he had a speech disorder as a youth and underwent surgery and speech therapy.

"I went to acting school, and at 19, I was in a play," he said. "Well, every line I said, I got a laugh. I later found out it was because my fly was open. So I left my fly open and became an actor."

But the two-time Oscar winner (for "Viva Zapta" in 1952 and "Lust for Life in 1956) and veteran of more than 100 films said he had not decided whether he is an actor yet. Quinn said he still feels he is in a learning process.

"I want a new life, another crack at it," the 67-year-old Quinn said.

When it comes to art, Quinn does more than act, Quinn is a sculptor, writer, painter and an architect—he currently is building a village in Italy.

And he collects art as well. Quinn said he began that endeavor at age 19 when he was very poor.

"I used to go by this antique shop, and there was a clay horse," he said. "I don't know what it was; I just liked it."

Later the shop owner, who had noticed Quinn looking through the window often, invited him inside. Quinn said he thought the man feared he might try to steal the figure.

"I told him some day I would own it," Quinn said. "It was $150. You know he asked me how much money I had. I dug in my pockets, and I had 35 cents. He took it as a down payment, and I paid for it for seven years."

He added that he recently was offered $300,000 for the clay horse.

"There is a great misunderstanding about what art is all about," the actor-artist said. "You cannot define art—I'm sorry to say this—as you cannot define God."

But he added, "A true artist is a prophet."

He also said the American artist is too unrealistic. "Americans have a watered-down version of the way life is," he said, making his point by giving examples of hit fantasy films such as "Star Wars" and "E.T."

"Americans have a tendency to not face reality," the outspoken Quinn contended.

When asked where he lives, Quinn said he had homes all over the world but remains a United States citizen: "I pay 70 percent of my income to American taxes. That way I have my right to protest. If I don't like something, then I can protest."

Clad in black trousers and a navy-blue pull-over shirt, Quinn also talked about his family and children, revealing that his 19-year-old son, Frank, had accompanied him on the trip. He later introduced his son to the audience.

"There are things that sons don't say to fathers and fathers don't say to sons," Quinn noted. "I'm glad that my son is here. Maybe he'll find out something he wanted to know."

He also said he did not want to raise his children in the United States, because of the "success syndrome" that he said is apparent in the American way of life.

Tarpon Springs Hails Greece's First Lady

By EMILY L. WILLIAMS
Sun staff writer

TARPON SPRINGS—More than 100 Tarpon Springs residents turned out Friday afternoon to honor Margaret Papandreou, wife of Prime Minister Andreas Papandreou of Greece.

During a 2:30 p.m. ceremony at St. Nicholas Greek Orthodox Church's community center, Mayor George Tsourakis gave Mrs. Papandreou the keys to the city and a certificate of honor. Prior to the ceremony, Mrs. Papandreou was guest of honor at a luncheon at Pappas Restaurant and visited the Sponge Docks, both on Dodecanese Boulevard.

"I'm in this country to make contact with Greek-American communities," Mrs. Papandreou told the crowd. "This government (Greek government) has a policy to make contact with the communities in the United States."

During her visit to the Sunshine State, she visited the EPCOT Center at Walt Disney World. "I was there to look into the possibilities

> Involved in politics since she was 12, Mrs. Papandreou is a founding member of the Panhellenic Liberation Movement in Greece and a member of its International Relations Committee.

of opening a Greek pavilion in EPCOT," she said. "However, I am not in a position to make these decisions. I am interested in the costs of such a project."

Also speaking at the reception were Father Tryfon Theofelopoulos of St. Nicholas, newly elected U.S. Rep. Michael Bilirakis and Julia Clones, economic minister of the Greek Embassy in Washington.

"To our first lady of Greece, I would like to say, in honor of the heritage, love and customs of Greece, I will do everything possible to keep our two countries together," Ninth District Rep. Bilirakis said.

Mrs. Papandreou was born in Oak Park, Ill., and met her husband while attending the University of Minnesota. They were married in 1951 and have three sons and one daughter. Their son George is a deputy in the Greek Parliament, Mrs. Papandreou said.

Photo by Emily W Skinner

Involved in politics since she was 12, Mrs. Papandreou is a founding member of the Panhellenic Liberation Movement in Greece and a member of its International Relations Committee.

In addition, she has written a book, "Nightmare in Athens" which describes her feelings about living under a dictatorial regime.

William Windom, a One-Man Class Act

When I saw a notice that William Windom was performing at the Asolo Theatre in Sarasota, I pitched an idea to the editor of a new national entertainment magazine publishing in Tampa Bay, *Comedy Magazine*. I was a fan of Windom's television show *My World and Welcome to It* and figured the humor of James Thurber (the TV show's focus) would be a nice throwback piece for the magazine. Windom, a well-known character actor was performing his one-man show of humorist James Thurber as well as World War II correspondent Ernie Pyle on alternating evenings. This seemed like a win for everyone. If I sold the article, I might help Windom sell tickets, the magazine's readers remember a forgotten wit, and myself, a glossy magazine credit.

What follows are the rough draft for *Comedy Magazine* and the actual Q&A interview transcribed from cassette tapes. The short article was a work in progress, written when I returned from the theater to get my visual notes down while they were fresh. I didn't have a commitment or assignment but felt I could tailor something if I had a word count and theme for a coming issue. The Windom interview seemed like a slam dunk to me. Florida's mature market loved interviews and articles about senior celebrities, but I hadn't considered *Comedy's* younger demographic. Ultimately, Windom wasn't a go with the editor, and sadly, the magazine didn't last long. A costly adventure for new publishers.

At the time, I was eight months pregnant and actively pitching and selling freelance articles wherever I could. I lived in Pinellas County and drove to Sarasota by what was then considered the long way (Gandy Bridge to U.S. 41) since the Skyway Bridge was under construction, having collapsed in 1980 when the Summit Venture freighter crashed into it. It was not something my family wanted me to do, especially not alone. I had taken my mother to see Windom's *Ernie Pyle II* the same week for an 8:15 pm show as my initial plan to secure the interview, so traveling back a second time solo during the day was not scary to me. But I did understand everyone's concerns.

Windom was tolerant of my retracing his roots and I believe enjoyed sharing his reasoning for bringing all four one-man shows to Sarasota. I learned quickly to plan interview questions (refer to Hank Williams, Jr. chapter) when I had an article idea I was convinced, I'd sold. In retrospect, I see obvious follow-up questions, knowing what I know now of actors and their challenge to keep working. The biggest a-ha was not asking why he didn't stick with the Thurber I show, since it was his bestseller. But I think I found the answer as I looked closely at his packaging of shows. Perhaps grant money or endowments paid Windom or a combination of box office and stipend. As such, shows could have meager attendance and Windom would still make his agreed upon fee or wage. By bundling shows, with his fame, university faculty would find his offerings attractive. With more opportunities, he'd have more stage time (which he enjoyed) and income.

Like most actors, Windom was obsessed with finding year-round work and probably would have been happy as a studio actor, but the era ended about the time he began. But then again, the studio system probably wouldn't have suited him as I imagine he'd probably have been critical of their restrictions. So he found a way to remain relevant, pay bills and tour the college circuit while awaiting film and television parts.

Though I didn't see it then, I was making things happen for myself, too. Often intimidated interviewing celebrities, I didn't let that stop me. I could make a fool of myself or be insulted by the interviewee, which happened with singer Melissa Manchester and Welsh actor Emlyn Williams (known for his one-man shows of Charles Dickens). Manchester had an activist agenda she wanted to discuss when I interviewed her, of which I was clueless until she brought it up. She said something like, "don't you have any better questions?" And Williams was not having my ignorance. I had never heard of him and didn't have much information to work with before our phone interview. So, I stuck with some essentials. Why did he choose acting … Why Dickens …What was next on the horizon…? His responses didn't provide much opportunity to follow up, either. No anecdotes. Just an air of frustration followed by something along the lines of stupid questions, and he shut down the call quickly. I was glad. It was torture for me, too. I still managed to stitch together a preview for his performance.

In these situations, the graphic designers enlarge the show still and fit the preview next to the image. And I didn't see Williams's show. The Welsh actor wouldn't answer enough questions and I didn't care to see him. And funny enough, I saw the new 2024 Faye Dunaway documentary on HBO Max, *Faye* where she talks about her big break on Broadway opposite Emlyn Williams. Well, well, I thought, here's old Scrooge himself. The ghost of Williams past (he died in 1987) on my television screen, a true Dickenson relic. And I also was in the room with Dunaway's ex-husband Peter Wolf (mentioned in the Bonomania chapter). Ultimately, I kept the Williams clip though I was tempted to trash it, and I had to keep Melissa Manchester's as a big spread for the portfolio. (See In Conclusion for these clips).

By comparison, Windom relished sharing his thoughts and backstory once he got going. Having perused the actor's 2009 self-published memoir, *Journeyman Actor*, I discovered my Q&A and belated interview have nuggets not included in his book. Ultimately, *Comedy Magazine* was looking for contemporary stand-up acts to fill their pages. The Windom interview didn't fit their format. It didn't stop me from feeling like I had lied, telling Windom he was going to be in the magazine. But it wasn't a lie, as I honestly felt I would find an angle as I was building a relationship with the magazine.

I promised to mail Windom the article, as he provided his Van Nuys home address. But I didn't have anything to send him, so I didn't follow up. I could have sent him a note, and continued to try to sell the piece, but ultimately, I lost focus once the magazine nixed the idea and my daughter was born.

As I listened to the interview, I enjoyed reliving our afternoon together. He was a pleasant guy. He even talked to my stomach, asking my chosen baby names. Which come to think of it is really special, knowing my daughter Marquel is an actor today. She had her first interaction with a professional artist in utero.

William Windom

His Big Break, Being An Only Child

A work in progress from an interview August 23, 1985
An unfinished freelance piece intended for *Comedy Magazine*
By Emily Skinner

Some may remember him for his role opposite Inger Stevens in *The Farmer's Daughter*, and others may associate actor William Windom with the Emmy-winning comedy series *My World and Welcome to It,* loosely based on the works of James Thurber, for which Windom scored an Emmy for acting. But no matter which role you like, Windom has firm opinions about the role he hopes will resound with his fans. When stopped by the public in airports or restaurants, the actor often produces a slip of paper with answers to questions he feels most people are going to ask him. "I was told once, that if I were to hand this to a reporter, he'd probably punch me," Windom said.

His films include, *To Kill A Mockingbird, The Americanization Of Emily, Mephisto Waltz, Fools Parade, Escape From The Planet Of The Apes*, and more. His Broadway credits are vast and comprise a number of roles. But when asked what he felt was his first big break, he answered, "Being an only child was the first break. It's essential if you want to get anywhere, at least in the use of the brain," he takes a breath and continues. "Most people with siblings spend their first, maybe, if they're lucky, 18 years squabbling about Barbie dolls. Some of them do it until they're fifty or worse. But if you come from a large day-to-day pettiness which most children go through…" something, which he was glad he missed. "Well, I got out of that by associating with adults. I spoke English properly. I read the *New York Times*. I was a teacher's pet. I was kind of precocious. Cost me a little bit of recess in some of the public schools in Virginia, but that's about all. I got smart after that."

A father of four, this 'break' didn't stop Windom from having just one child. "I was determined to have more and make it work better," he explained. Leaning back in his chair, hands folded resting on his head, the 62-year-old actor appears comfortable yet somewhat adamant. Questions seem to bore him. He wants conversation. Or maybe he is running lines in this head? Behind the pale blue eyes, it seems that there is much on this man's mind. Doing two shows a day for a four-day run to benefit the Asolo State Theater in Sarasota requires some mental gymnastics. This was the first time Windom brought all four of his one-man shows, Thurber I & II and Ernie Pyle I & II, together in one city.

Windom has toured with the one-man shows for thirteen years and isn't bored by it. In fact, he says he enjoys them even more. Performing roughly forty shows a year, he has played all but four states, Utah, New Mexico, Montana and Rhode Island. When asked if he preferred theater to television his response was an immediate yes. "It doesn't pay that much, but it is more fun to do." He was quick to state it is hard to get work performing live.

Of the work he is most proud, he answers the one-man shows. Of his television credits, he said, "I bought one copy of a TV show that I did in 1970. Actually, so that when the kids are old enough to speak English, they can see what the old man used to do. It was a segment of *Night Gallery*, 'They're Tearing Down Tim Riley's Bar.' He goes on, "There are some people who think that the acme of my career was playing Commodore Decker in *Star Trek*. He explained that he liked *Star Trek*. "What I don't like is people say wow weren't you excited to do that (*Star Trek*). Come on... What are you giving me? It's okay. It's no big deal. Don't give everything first prizes. They do tend to give everything the first prize."

Restlessly, Windom moves about in his chair. We've talked for a good 30 minutes. He is ready to move to another location. He suggests a small restaurant on the Ringling Museum's grounds, just a short stretch from the theater. Walking over he seems more at ease. His attire is casual, navy-blue shorts, red pullover and baby blue deck shoes which just fit his swollen feet.

Once in the restaurant, he talks about his children ages 20, 15, 13 and 7. He also talks about his wife, who was in a recent car accident and broke her neck. He explains that she has to wear a halo brace screwed into her skull which is attached to a form with straps around her upper torso. His wife's condition concerns him a great deal. And he plans to meet her and the children in New York, after he closes in Sarasota for a short cruise to take their minds off things for a little while.

As more people enter the restaurant, they begin to recognize the familiar face. A gentleman with his wife and two children approached Windom for an autograph as he was leaving the restaurant. "Mr. Windom, you were on *My World and Welcome to It*," the man says. Windom chats for a moment and signs a Ringling brochure the man has handed him. Once the family was gone, "Now he would have done that better had he been alone," Windom notes. "People are more intelligent and handle themselves better when they're not in a crowd." Bringing to mind a missed question, did he ever consider directing?

F IS FOR FICTION

Asolo State Theater℠ 1984-85 Season *Presents*

WILLIAM WINDOM

in his Internationally Acclaimed One Man Shows

Thurber I
Thurber II
Ernie Pyle I
Ernie Pyle II

WILLIAM WINDOM, the Emmy Award-winning star of TV's "My World And Welcome To It" plus 22 Broadway hits and countless films, brings his internationally acclaimed One Man Shows on Ernie Pyle and James Thurber to Asolo for a limited engagement only. Reserve Now!

August 20 - 23 only - at Asolo Theater

JAMES THURBER, like Mark Twain, was an American original; a humorist whose laughter has become part of our lives. In short stories and fables, cartoons of flappy-eared hounds, matronly women, and balding intellectuals; in plays, books, and the New Yorker Magazine, he poked magnificent fun at our foibles. WILLIAM WINDOM is a "Thurber Carnival" rolled into two shows, drawn from different Thurber material. Both are hilarious; enjoy them alone or in tandem.

ERNIE PYLE was a newspaper man who, in the 1930s and 40s, wrote a column a day for the Scripps-Howard chain. They weren't about sports or politics; they WERE about the GI, the dogface. Pyle wrote about these kids in every theater of World War II until he died in the South Pacific. Windom also tells about Pyle's pre-War travels across America, and you and I come out looking pretty okay. Ernie Pyle I concentrates on England and North Africa; Pyle II takes us into the Pacific. Both are funny and sad, honest and uproarious. See them both!

Location: The Asolo Theater
Times: Thurber I - August 20 at 8:15 PM, August 22 at 2 PM; Thurber II - August 21 at 2 PM, August 23 at 8:15 PM; Ernie Pyle I - August 20 at 2 PM, August 22 at 8:15 PM; Ernie Pyle II - August 21 at 8:15 PM, August 23 at 2 PM.
Prices: Matinees: **$7, $12, $14**; Sunday thru Thursday Evenings: **$10, $12, $15**; Friday and Saturday Evenings: **$11, $13, $16**. *(Asolo Angels and Curtain Raisers receive 10% discount on these prices).* Major credit cards accepted.
FOR RESERVATIONS, call the Asolo Box Office at Sarasota **355-5137**; visit the Box Office at the Ringling Museums, or write Asolo, Postal Drawer E, Sarasota, FL 33578.

Photo of program by Emily W. Skinner

William Windom Interview August 23, 1985

Asolo Repertory Theatre on the grounds of
Ringling Museum of Art in Sarasota

WW: There's a picture I think you want to see on the way out. A commercial I do here in Florida and there's a picture of me which is the way I think I look, which is kind of fun. (We forgot to look.)

EW: As a child you traveled with your flapper parents to Europe four times. What did they do?

WW: My father was an architect, and my mother was a southern belle. She was born in Montgomery, AL raised in Virginia.

EW: You were born and raised in New York?

WW: No, I was born in New York and raised primarily in Europe and Virginia and Massachusetts and Connecticut.

EW: And you moved back to New York when you were in your twenties. What made you decide on an acting career?

WW: It looked easy.

EW: Did you study acting?

WW: No. I mean you never stop studying. But I never paid for any lessons.

EW: What was your first big break?

WW: Being an only child was the first break first. That's essential if you want to get anywhere at least in the use of the brain. Most people with siblings spend their first 18 years squabbling about Barbie dolls. Some do it until they're 50, or worse. If you come from a large Italian family chances are you'll be an adult when you're 9 or 10. But if you have the American ideal, quote background, Dagwood and Blondie. Then you're going to be stuck with it for a long time.—Give me that. That's mine. He took. She took. I want. Gimme. Gimme. Gimme. I'm horrified at what I see. Well, I got out of that plan having associated with adults accordingly. I spoke English properly. I read the New York Times. I was a teacher's pet. I was kind of precocious. Cost me a little bit of recess in some of the public schools in Virginia, but that's about all. I got smart after that. Uh, you don't have to follow the bullies' path in order to abate the bully.

EW: How many children do you have?

WW: I have four.

EW: You weren't going to have just one?

WW: (Laughs) I get that all the time. I was determined to have more and make it work better. The two older ones are coming out of it. One of them is twenty and she's been out of it. She's been an adult in that sense. The fifteen-year-old is gonna make it in a couple more years. The thirteen and seven are still just as dumb as any America.

EW: Did your parents encourage your performance?

WW: No. Well, I mean they never discouraged it. But they certainly didn't push me into being an architect. In fact, my father said don't do that, that's terrible. And I see what he means on the other hand, he would have had a difficult life whatever he chose because he drank too much. He was one of those guys. Which also made him very sensitive and very clever, and very witty. (inaudible) that particular generation, Hemingway, Fitzgerald. The lost generation. The flappers. Yeah, well they went through a whole lot. They were filled with such hopes when World War I started. They were going to solve the whole problem. Then it all came unglued. Then the depression came. Then it was you know. They really went through so much. I've always liked those people. My parents' contemporaries.

EW: Is that why you chose the era (referring to his one-manshows)?

WW: Possibly. Possibly that.

EW: What was your first break into show business? Was it the New York stage?

WW: No, it was before that. It was in the army after the war was over. I conned my way into a college that they formed over there for guys waiting to come home. As a gag, you know just to get out of Frankfurt Germany and over to France where we could see some more people. Maybe meet some new girls. You know young guys. The war's over. We're ready to go. They put on a play, and we got thrown out of the first audition. We're going to meet all the girls there to be actresses. You know hot stuff, right? They tossed us out of the first audition. Thanks very much. What the hell is that? You know, come on. So, we went to the second audition and when the time came, they read off all the names and we weren't there. What do you mean? We're here for the second audition, sir. What're your names? Windom and Johnson, sir.—You're not on the list. But sir, we've been waiting for two hours. They told us, you know.—Okay, go on in. Same old thing. Kids are good at that.

EW: Yeah.

WW: Yeah, (laughs) once in there we each got a part in the show. I was playing Richmond, comes in later, the last act. My buddy was playing King Edward the 4th. Gets killed in the first act. We're gonna have the whole second act to boost the girls (boost their egos). Gonna be great. So, we get around to the first reading. Richard Whorf is gonna play Richard. He's going to direct it. Big hotshot Hollywood, New York director when he comes in about three sheets to the wind (intoxicated). He says all right men I have to go back and direct a picture with Fernando Llamas and Esther Williams. I will be in the state... (inaudible) I will direct it. I will do the sets for you. Get you started here. Then, I've got to get back to Hollywood. Lieutenant Fisher is going to play Richard. Go Fisher, go ahead and read it. Fisher got about ohh halfway through that first speech and Whorf was pacing up... mumbling to himself. He said, "Stop. Stop. Give me that. He hands it to the next kid. He gets about six lines out. Stop. He hands it to the next kid. Well, I'm the fourth kid down the line. He let me get about six lines. He says, stop. I hand it to the next guy. He says, what's your name? Windom, sir. What part are you playing? Richmond, sir. Okay. Uh huh. Fisher, you're playing Richmond. Windom you're playing Richard. The reason for that is. Only child. Speaks English. I don't say 'and, uh.' And also, I had some great aunts who made me read Shakespeare when I was 11, and report on it at lunch every day up in Massachusetts. I had to read selections from it. They did not allow the phrase 'and, uh' either. I got the job as

Richard. The show was a success. And I thought this (acting) looks like a snap. Got a couple of breaks and here I still am.

EW: I think people who started out I guess in the 40s. A lot of them did not study acting. I interviewed Cesar Romero. He said the same thing. He never took an acting class. He was just interested and went out there.

WW: A gorgeous Latin. A nice guy, too.

EW: Your three-year stint in the business world. What did you do?

WW: I bought insurance.

EW: Was that in New York?

WW: Yes.

EW: Is that when you were pondering your career?

WW: It was when I first got married. I needed some money. I couldn't get a (acting) job, by the way, for the first year. I really didn't know how to look for one. I began to have doubts about whether I should be an actor. I would still have those doubts had I not done that three years in the insurance business. Nothing wrong with it. Is a good business, but it's a business. It's a nine to five collar and tie business. And most things are in the normal WASP (White Angelo-Saxon Protestant) world 9 to 5— stock broker, lawyer doctor, engineer. I'd rather work two shows a day for four days. Maybe 12 hours a day on television when I can get it, then 9:00 to 5:00 in an office. What you miss, of course, is security and the sense of purpose and direction in your life. That, I'm glad to say, I don't need anymore. If I'd never done that (worked in insurance), I would have always been slightly dubious that I had made the wrong decision.

EW: I have that you were in New York during the 40s, 50s, and 60s.

WW: Yes, I got my first job there in '46 and I left there in '61, right. And I went to California.

EW: What was New York like in those days?

WW: It was my hometown.

EW: Thurber and EB White, and all these people spent time together at the Algonquin…

WW: That was all over before I got there. That would have been over in the early, ohh late 40s.

EW: Do you prefer theater to television?

WW: It doesn't make as much money but it's more fun to do.

EW: Did you become acquainted (meet) with Thurber?

WW: I read a lot of people.

EW: Do you feel Thurber (referring to his one-manshows) is more commercially acceptable than Pyle?

WW: I do.

EW: Do you prefer Thurber or Pyle better?

WW: Pyle, but it's harder to sell. It's a younger show. It's like raising children. Thurber can play by itself. Thurber II sturdy fellow, selling nicely. Ernie Pyle needs a little help, and Pyle II is really just a baby. It needs a lot of encouragement.

EW: You know when I first called up about coming to the show. I didn't know that there were four shows, because when they first advertised it. It just said Thurber and Pyle. I thought the first act was one (Thurber) and then the second was the next (Pyle). Well, I saw Pyle II. So, did you travel with the two shows?

WW: I travel with all four shows, but I only sell people Thurber II if they bought Thurber I. I don't sell Ernie Pyle II, unless they bought Pyle I.

EW: (I didn't follow up with the fact that I saw Pyle II)

WW: Ernie Pyle II, since 1976, has only sold five shows… tells you …let's say 35 or 40 of them (audiences) have been to Pyle I. Only five of those people repeated. Whereas Thurber I has sold upwards of 500 (performances) and has only sold about 85 Thurber IIs gives you about the percentage.

EW: So, you prefer which style of writing?

WW: Mr. Thurber had more time. Mr. Thurber lived a more urban life. A city boy, he chose to mingle with more people who were very articulate. Pyle chose to mingle with people who were as common as dirt. He also mingles with the big shots but basically, he was a folk writer. One works for The New Yorker (Thurber), the other works for Scripps Howard (Pyle).

EW: What selections are in your Thurber show, because I didn't get to see that one.

WW: You gotta stay. Today or tonight? You can't stay over?

EW: If it was 2:00.

WW: It'll be around. I do short stories obviously. One serious in each act, mostly comedic stuff, fables and drawings on the slide. He was quite a skillful caricaturist. He didn't think so.

EW: E.B. got him (Thurber) started. I think he (Thurber) did like 30 a day, just these little drawings and handing them out. I think my favorite I've read of his (short stories) is his 10 rules (10 Rules To A Happy Marriage).

WW: That's a good one. I only use three of the rules.

EW: You've been doing these shows for thirteen years.

WW: Yeah, I started in '72. At the end of the year, I'll start year 14.

EW: Do you still enjoy doing them just as much?

WW: If not more, Well, it isn't steady. I only do about 40 shows a year, so it isn't a grind that way. If I would have been playing this show on Broadway, all one-manshows, all together, it would run for just over a year, instead of 15. So, I do about one show every two weeks on average.

EW: How many states have you traveled to?

WW: All but four. Well, I missed two of those states, Utah and I missed New Mexico and the other two are Montana and Rhode Island which really makes me mad. It's one of the old ones. I mean you can understand Utah, New Mexico. Montana. What the hell, nobody there anyway. But Rhode Island! That's disgusting. I've got Hawaii and Alaska got down. Alaska!

EW: What kind of audience did you have in Alaska?

WW: Normal people. They spend $18.00 for lunch instead of $6. Everything is higher up there.

EW: Do you think it is important to keep the humor of that era alive?

WW: Or any other era. Humor is fun. Humor is good. They have to be pretty good. At least Thurber, Pyle isn't so humorous. He has some funny stuff, but it's more reflective.

EW: What do you like most about Pyle, the man?

WW: His sensitivity. He was really quick. He was a gentler, kinder man. That would be my guess, but they were equally sensitive.

EW: How did you choose Pyle?

WW: I wanted to do something on World War II. Somebody hired me to do anything I wanted to do, except Thurber. They said you got eight months. You don't even have to memorize anything. I don't wanna do Washington or Harry Truman. The only thing I ever took seriously in my life was World War II. I'll just get him (he doesn't identify him) an evening of that.

Windom considered doing *Catch 22* or selections from *The Young Lions*.

WW: I was beginning to assemble that wondering how the hell am I gonna pay these guys (Joseph Heller for *Catch 22* or Irwin Shaw for *The Young Lions*) to use their stuff on stage? They're all gonna want a slice of the pie. There'll not be much left. And while I'm researching, it was good stuff, too. I could still do it, but it's fiction and I stumbled on the book of Pyle's. And wait a minute… There's a guy that wrote it down. Here's the diarist of World War II. It's not as sharp, mean and hard as I wanted it to be. Like from *Young Lions*, I was going to put stuff in there. It really would cut your hair, but it's genuine and people would like it better. Another thing to do for example, the one I wanted to put in in *Young Lions* was a scene where some American infantry are dug in on the hillside overlooking Cologne. The Roer River, down in front, snowing cold. It's a part of the war that I know about. I was in that part of the falls area. And they're dug in and they're miserable and they're only about four guys left in each twelve-man company… (I have removed Windom's retelling of *The Young Lions*. To paraphrase, it involved infantry men sacrificing two fellow soldiers who show up at a convenient time.) It's a fiction story by Irwin Shaw. But it should have happened, if it didn't, because that's the way we felt. That's the way I felt. They didn't rotate the infantry. If you were in the infantry, you either died or you got taken prisoner or you got wounded. You weren't going to get sent back to rest. I mean, you get sent back for a couple of days to rest but then you're back in the line. The pilots got 30 missions. They go home to the states, or 35 (missions) or whatever it was. Others (infantry)…no, go you're dumb. You're the low figure on the totem pole. Go and die for us.

EW: You were in the infantry.

WW: Yes. They did it to the guys in Vietnam. Even worse. And they did it to the guys in Korea. It's near me, you know. I didn't like it in World War II. And supposedly everybody was behind us. Everybody said ohh yes, our boys are wonderful. Let's go. As Pyle points out, there are twenty guys behind the lines for every one that's getting shot in the infantry. Twenty guys, truck drivers, cooks, clerks, artillery, flyers, supply and they're all in the service. And they're all getting medals.

Windom feels strongly about the military's lack of concern for the infantry. He continues.

WW: Well, you should rotate him in my opinion, right. My opinion is that. So, to point that out. Here's the story of how they got even (referring to *Young Lions)*. At least once. Just once. You call it murder if you want. It's perfectly simple to call that murder. It is murder, right? It's murder, you know you get to a point finally. And I had very little time relatively speaking in the industry. I went into combat on September 17th of 44 and I came out two months later. And then I went into the Bulge (Battle of the Bulge) for about one or two, maybe three or four weeks. Maybe a total of three months in what you call combat. That doesn't mean you're being fired at all the time. But you're up in the line for three months and three months that's nothing to the guys who don't have for three years or better. Germans did it for six or seven years. So finally, if you stay there long enough and it can be as short a time as two or three hours.

You begin to think, well yeah, this is what it is. This is what I wanted to know. I found out but I don't like the guy who's 50 yards behind me sitting in a warmer place. And I really don't like the guy who's a mile behind me who's lying down in the bed and the guy has passed. I don't care about anybody behind them. The guy I really am feeling sympathy toward is a poor young kraut (German) who's right across from me. He's catching the same shit I am, and he's got fat asses behind him, too. I know he does. So, we're the two losers. We're the two that are gonna die first. And we're living in the worst conditions. And we're the youngest. We should have a better chance than we're getting. And behind us are lardasses… getting bigger.

As you go back further, well this is a speculative dream. You don't go up and say, hey kid (the enemy). Let's stick together. Although they did it a couple of times in World War I, I'm told. They got punished for it, too. But we didn't do that because we really hated the krauts (Germans). That was the reason we hate them. That's all it was. Just like dealing with animals as far as we were concerned. But your instincts were …also, you protect the guys next to you. Those are your only friends in the whole wide world. With people next to you. The ones behind you don't mean much, and the ones in front of you are out to kill you. You got some friends next to you, maybe. And if they're ten yards back, they're not as close a friend as the guy who's really with him. That's how the emotions work.

So accordingly, that's why I wanted to set that up for the show. There's that one *Catch 22* has got a lot of that. Going forward also it's done with the Air Force. Young, young, young life was loaded with it. What's that one that (Norman) Mailer did? The first one he did? It was kind of a good patrol story, I forgot. *The Naked and the Dead,* and *Naked* in the day and then *From Here to Eternity,* of course was the Hawaiian thing, which was okay. The best war story I ever saw on film, anyway, was something that MGM did years ago called *Red Badge of Courage.* It had to do with the Civil War. It had to do with two guys who were privates in the Union Army and all you saw was the war from their point of view. A lot of trees. A lot of firing in the distance. A general galloping by. Guys with guns running toward… Running back. You never saw anything. Just total utter confusion, fear and horror. Hey, are you here? What am I doing here? I'm 19 years old. That was a true war story, I thought. And you know what they use? They use Audie Murphy and Bill Mauldin to play those two parts. It was a classic piece of work. Got written up in *The New Yorker* as a bad example of filmmaking, but I don't think it was. I thought it was a very good example. It only ran about an hour an hour and five minutes. Wasn't a long film. Wasn't a long story.

EW: Do you find that audiences in retired states like Florida accept Pyle?

WW: They're no different in Florida than they are in college. There's no audience that would like that scene I just described to you (regarding *The Young Lions*), except possibly some guys in prison might like it. College now Pyle gets into enough of that with the true stuff, so that you get the flavor of it without having really gone overboard.

EW: Is your audience (for one-manshows) primarily college students?

WW: Yes.

EW: Is there anything of which you are particularly proud?

WW: A television work. I bought one copy of a TV show that I did in 1970. Actually, so that when the kids are old enough to speak English, they can see what the old man used to do. There was a segment of *Night Gallery*, and it was called "They're Tearing Down Tim Riley's Bar."

EW: I know, I saw that. But I can't remember it.

WW: Maybe so and if you can't remember it didn't affect you that much. So, it doesn't work in your case. It isn't worth looking up. But in mine it was. And that isn't necessarily bad, one man's meat is another man's poison. There are some people who think that the acme of my career was playing Commodore Decker in *Star Trek*. To them that was thrilling. There are other people who say *My World and Welcome to It*. It was a damn good show. It got the award.

EW: They don't rerun some of these shows.

WW: No. They didn't rerun that one. There's not enough, 26 episodes. I like *Star Trek*. What I don't like is people say wow weren't you excited to do that (*Star Trek*). Come on, it's just another God damn TV show. What are you giving me? It's okay. It's no big deal. Don't give everything first prizes. They do tend to give everything the first prize.

EW: In your statement, you said you more or less have been able to support your family through your work. How do you feel your career has fared?

WW: Okay. I work about half the time.

EW: You do just what you want?

WW: No, I don't. I don't do half as much as what I want. I wish I could do twice as much as I do.

EW: The work isn't available.

WW: That's right. Or I'm not available for it. You lose ground by being too young, which I was for the first ten years in my career. Then I was just right for about 40 minutes. Then after that I was always too old. Again, the Italian family, a little boy of twelve who is an adult Italian of 12 and looks the same and weighs the same and stays the same until he's 85, he can work from 10 to 85 looking the same way playing gangsters the whole way through and everybody buys it. But with an Anglo-Saxon mushy face like mine, which is like George Peppard or for some other like Reagan's. Reagan's got a mushy face, too. We fade out awful fast as far as that is concerned. And when you get older or fatter or whatever it is you lose parts. They want the young studs for the sexy stuff just like they want the young girls for the sexy stuff. They're not too interested in character women. It depends… is an area of gee I wish I was doing that, tends to be what sells tickets. Gee I wish

I was doing that is about where the money is. So, if you have a Rhett Butler or Marilyn Monroe or even the comics can do it for a while, or gorgeous ice skater or, even a fine ballerina. Everything is right there. At the Acme of their sexual prowess. Is where they're working them. Where they're making the money. Why? Because the people sitting in the dark say, *Gee I wish I was doing that*. Kind of sad.

EW: You were in a recent episode of *Highway to Heaven* and that was a faster character. Which roles do you enjoy?

WW: I liked that one very much, because I thought it had something to say. It made sense to me. I mean the guy was a little bit rough on his daughter but then there are people who do that. They're not all kind to their daughters. So, within that framework, he thought he'd been handed the shaft by his daughter. And he was hot. He was upset. But the storyline, which was written directed, produced and acted in by Michael Landon. Whom I never thought that much of before, I thought he was okay. He never was a plus or minus but he's a real plus in my book now. That guy works hard and does a good job and does it well. And the favorite thing I noticed about him. They have in California what's known as a Honeywagon, which is a long trailer with maybe 6 dressing rooms in it which consists of a couch and a mirror and a toilet and that's where each actor has his head, hangs up his clothes and gets dressed and sits or sleeps, whatever he's been doing between the shots. It's his own room. Like a baby stateroom, called the Honeywagon. And they have those usually for all the actors, and then for the stars and the director and other people, they have a motorhome, which has a kitchenette … you know a regular thing—motorhome. On the set of *Highway to Heaven* there was a double set of Honeywagons, Michael Landon has one of those little cubicles, and whoever else. Nobody gets anything fancy. They all get a little cell. Okay. Okay, baby. (Taps on table) You got it. That's nice.

EW: You don't prefer comedy to drama?

WW: No, I don't prefer one over the other. I think comedy is more exacting. It takes more effort and skill. It's fun. I like to make people laugh. I don't want to make people cry all the time, but I have to give a little variety. (He offers) You want some coffee? You want to split a cup of black coffee? Or you're not you're not supposed to have any?

EW: (I'm pregnant) I can't have it.

WW: Well, you can't. I'll get you something else. We'll go over to the thing. (Café at the Ringling) If you wanna go now. We can go over to the over there and get a bowl of soup or something. Would you like to do that?

EW: I'd be happy to.

WW: I don't have to be back here until about 1:00, it's 11:45 a.m. so we've got all the time we need. Let's finish this up here and then go over. Okay? Let's do that.

EW: I just got a few more questions. Are there any television shows or anything you have in the works coming up?

WW: I may get to do a couple more *Murder, She Wrote*. She's cute. She's awfully sweet.

EW: Where is home to you now?

WW: I live in Los Angeles; a suburb called Van Nuys.

EW: How do you feel about being interviewed?

WW: Well, it depends on the interviewer. That sheet I gave you, covers, again, 90% of what the interviewers usually want to know. And if they've read that and they want to talk more, I'm happy too. I like people. I'm gregarious. And there are people who do interviewing that are fun. Sometimes they're nervous if they're 15 or 18 in college. Or sometimes they're blase and know it all. They're all trying. Some are a little more aggressively… trying to write an unpleasant review. I'm not going to understand why. That makes sense to some of them. Because there was a time when I wanted to be a reviewer, too. I wanted to review pictures or plays. I still may do it when I get older. It's kind of a fun thing to do, because then they can't say well, he couldn't be an actor, so he became a reviewer. No, no, I've finished all that now, I'm reviewing you. Pay attention because I got you, brother. I'm gonna be laughing.

EW: Do you want any of your kids to go into show business?

WW: No. (inaudible) Chances are no, but who knows. If they do, I'll help them. There's a lot of misery.

EW: It seems like it would be very lonely.

WW: I mean working is fine. I love working. If you're working, you're fine. But it's the out of work, most actors,—my union will tell you that in the heyday of Hollywood there were what 7000 members of the Screen Actors Guild back in the days of *Gone With the Wind*. And they get about 1000 new members a year and drop about 1000. But it always stays at about 7000. And, oh 80% of them are working and making a living. Now it's up to 58,000 and there may be twice as many jobs but there are 58,000 people trying for them. And the average income is about I think it's $800 a year. Five percent of them are those 58,000 that take 90% of the billing. That's the Sinatras, the Liberaces, that's the product the public is buying. That's the product they choose. That's what you get. The others are scrambling just to stay alive.

EW: So, you have to get into the commercials, as well.

WW: Whatever, I'm just taking it, an overall picture because let's say you can bring up your average for the entire—for all three unions: Screen Actors, Television actors, Stage actors … it dovetails a lot. There're people in all three. In fact, I'm in all three. Let's say there are 75,000 actors in all three unions. Well, their average income is probably under $1,000 a year. That means they're working maybe half a week a year on the average out of 52 weeks. They're working 1% of the time. Can't live on that. If you're single you could probably live on 20 weeks a year. If you're married, you've gotta look for 45 to 50 weeks a year.

EW: Unreal.

WW: It is unreal. And everybody who sees you believes you're loaded and … they figure anybody on TV has it made.

EW: They think the same way about anybody who writes.

WW: (Laughs) You must be loaded.

Fun poses Windom suggested.
Photos by Emily W Skinner
William Windom

Me at Hank Williams, Jr. concert
Photo by Jackie Lott

Hank Williams, Jr.

I don't think Hank done it this way

Hank Williams, Jr, concert
Lakeland Civic Center
Unpublished
Friday, November 6, 1981

The crowd was clad in country and western hats, blue jeans, rhinestones, cowboy boots, plaid flannel, gingham long sleeve shirts, fringed suede jackets and sunburned faces. Resident Marlboro men were accompanied by a mix of heavily made-up ladies, Ivory soap models, and well-behaved offspring. They smelled of woodsy soap and cologne, unlike rock concert fans that smell of a mix of marijuana, Patchouli oil, spilled beer and sometimes vomit. Country or Western men (is there always an "and") marked their territory in Brut, Hai Karate, and Old Spice aftershave. Epitomizing Hank's new release, "All My Rowdy Friends (Have Settled Down)," these early to bed early to rise types simply wanted to hear a couple hours of Williams singing, then drive their pick-up trucks, semi cabs or the wife's Pontiac GTO home and go to sleep. Unfamiliar to me, was the blue-collar intolerance of unruly yahoos. *Dukes of Hazard,* they were not.—Disruptive behaviors got steely-eyed *take it down a notch* or take it outside glances. Lost was the spontaneous yeehaw, awkward dances, and redneck toasts

I'd expected to partake in. Instead, everyone sat the entire show like seat-fillers at the Country Music Awards. You'd thought they were giving prizes for manners.

As the resident Mass Communications major in the room, I contained my own whoop and holler and decided to take action of another kind. I spied Williams's cowboy security detail guarding the stage and devised a plan. Beforehand, I told my friends I would be back. They watched me like, *Is she alright?* My heart bounced in my ribcage. I was hoping Hank wouldn't spy me leaving my seat. I was sure a net would drop, capture me and whisk me into the backseat of a sheriff's cruiser. I strolled down to the stage *like this is normal* and had a conversation with one of the cowpokes and said loudly into his ear. "I want to interview Hank after the show." He nodded. I was not expecting an affirmative. We were in a zone. He said loudly in my ear, "I didn't say this but, Hank's heading to the Grist Mill in Polk County to do a jam session. If you show up there, I'll get you in."

Hot damn! I couldn't believe my strained eardrums. A gut instinct had finally paid off (unlike the time I tried to blow bubbles into a full milk bottle, reference my novel *The Movie Queen*). I nodded. Said I'd see him there. It was that easy. Seriously, that easy! Staples office supply didn't become a brand until 1986, so there was no *Easy Button* in 1981.

I went back to my seat and told my best friend and she told her husband and then I told my date about the rendezvous. Everyone was on board. I couldn't wait for the concert to end. I don't think I heard anything other than loud(er) ringing in my ears (which I've had since third grade—but not as loud). I was excited.

Global Positioning Systems (GPS) didn't exist then. Paper maps, really good directions from random people, and perhaps an aftermarket compass ball glued to center of a car's dashboard, plus gut instinct were the way of travel, unless you were going great distances, then you might order a *AAA Triptik* booklet of paper maps that flip like scavenger hunt clues. *Triptiks* were astonishingly accurate. Anyway, we discreetly asked a few locals after the concert for tips on how to get to the bar and then tore off into the night.

Cue up the *Smokey and the Bandit* soundtrack. Unlit backroads led to a well-lit interstate highway and then back to the darkness as our headlights searched for edges of pavement, occasionally skidding atop soft-shouldered ditches as we raced like moonshiners escaping the law. Would we make it to the honky-tonk promised land? Everyone was excited. We didn't even consider this might have been a diversion tactic by Williams security to mislead crazed fans.

Then the thought hit me. *What if we actually find the place?*

We found the bar!

Outside of the lounge was a white stretch limousine. My friends were excited for me. I got out of their car and walked over to the security cowboy from the show. He nodded to me. I approached. He said, "Hank's inside," with a head click toward the limo. "You'll get ten minutes and then he's going in to jam."

Waylon Jennings said it best, "No I don't think Hank done 'em this a'way."

Security opened the limo door and I jumped into the darkness. There, seated across from me was Hank and a lady friend. I plopped down. Hank wore his signature sunglasses. His shirt was unbuttoned mostly. His long legs were clad in some kind of show wear, not jeans and now his knees were touching my knees. His left arm draped over the woman's shoulder. She wore a slinky top or dress with a lot of cleavage showing. I tried not to look at her. The two of them stared at me. Was the limo's air conditioning working? Why was it so hot? Could they see my face redden? I could barely see their faces in the darkness. I hadn't thought of a single question. My mind was blank. I started yammering about his daddy, Hank Sr. ... and God knows what. This space capsule was running out of oxygen. I went for the escape hatch—excused myself, said my time was up and got out.

My friends were proud. You'd think I'd gone the distance with a prize fighter. I was certainly beating myself up for what amounted to two minutes self-talk. The guy who let me into the limo looked at me like, *you got enough?*

Well, I had had enough.

Lillian Gish Talks To Admirers About Film History

16 Page, The Southcoaster
November 26, 1981
By EMILY L. WILLIAMS

Lillian Gish, one of the first ladies of American Film, appeared last Thursday evening before a packed house in St. Petersburg Junior College's auditorium.

Ms. Gish, known for the many D.W. Griffith films she appeared in, spoke to the crowd of her film career, past and present. The petite movie star dressed in a long evening gown, greeted her audience with open arms. Shortly after her introduction the lights were dimmed as all watched the film by John Gartenberg, that featured clips from many of her memorable performances, including silent films "Broken Blossoms," "The Wind", and "Night of the Hunter," directed by Charles Laughton, as well as her most recent film, Robert Altman's "A Wedding."

Ms. Gish also appeared in D.W. Griffith's 1915 film classic, "Birth of a Nation." A film described by SPJC's film instructor, Bill Gamage, as being the first significant feature length film. Gammage, as many of his students know, teaches the foundations of Griffith's experimental camera angles (that are used so often in films today) and says that in teaching Griffith, he teaches Gish.

Photo of article by Emily W Skinner

Gammage was instrumental in bringing Lillian Gish to the college. It was Gammage who suggested Gish to the Lyceum Committee and personally contacted her. Sending a letter and a single rose, he believes the rose is what lured her. He also arranged for a 1935 white Rolls Royce to pick her up at Tampa International Airport and another late model Rolls to transport her on her brief visit to the St. Petersburg area, both at his expense.

Earlier that morning, Ms. Gish lectured for an equally large audience of SPJC students, faculty, and other invited guests, stating the only acting lesson she ever had was "speak loud and clear or they'll get another little girl."

The 85-year-old actress and her sister, Dorothy, began their acting careers in the theater and later were discovered by Griffith, who cast them in motion pictures. Ms. Gish said in films if you

Inspiration

To my surprise Lillian Gish made a cameo in my novel *Mind Hostage*. Seeing her in person and watching her film *Way Down East* impressed me so much that it became an integral part of my novel's plot. I didn't set out to include Gish's character in the novel but rather my characters saw her film and were affected by the tragedy, much the same as I was. My characters are not me, but they do share my knowledge. This is the mystical part of writing. *Mind Hostage* started as Suzy's narrative but became a multi-generational tale whereby Lillian Gish as Anna Moore in *Way Down East* becomes a key that unlocks a mystery within a mystery. That's where the story took me. It differed from my original outline but still concluded as plotted. Thank you, Lillian.

"get caught acting, they don't believe you." And she feels sure that silent films will come back, stating that "... they're not even a century old yet."

Ms. Gish's beauty is still alive as her youthful personality. The only difference is that Father Time has permitted a few wrinkles, but no loss of memory. She candidly recalls incidents and directors she has worked with and the processes of creating certain films. For example, in the movie "The Wind," eight airplanes propellors were used to create the tremendous wind storm. In "Way Down East," they had to wait three weeks before weather conditions were right for travel to White Water Junction to shoot the final scene on the ice as it floated down the river. And in most cases only one take of each scene could be shot, due to budget and weather on location.

In a short question and answer period, a student asked Ms. Gish if her film "Way Down East" was ever subject to censorship, due to the fact that she had an illegitimate baby in the 1920 movie. She said strongly, "I had it (the baby) every place but Philadelphia, they wouldn't allow it."

At the closing of Thursday night's guest appearance, Ms. Gish thanked three young men in the audience for sending her a bouquet of orchids while she was staying at the Don CeSar Hotel, by giving them each a kiss.

The Murderer

"Adolescence is one of the most dramatic and formative periods of our lives. It is when we become who we are, when the smallest things can have life-long effects. But it is also full of contradictions, making it bewildering to live through and widely misunderstood."

—Coming of Age: The Life-Long Impact of Adolescence, welldoing.org

I wrote an essay for my SPJC (St. Petersburg Junior College) Mass Communications class titled, *Sometimes, We Don't Just Meet By Chance* about an acquaintance who eventually murdered a young couple about my same age when I met him. The title implied pre-destination might play a part in how our lives intersect. Sounds heady I know. But as a Catholic, I tend to look at everything as why? I often ask God, "why am I experiencing, hearing or seeing this?" God's been nagging me about this story for a long time. It's not something I ever wanted to tell my kids. My husband said I should've written a true crime manuscript—long before murder was in vogue on social media and content streaming. Today the macabre has become somewhat kitsch. Take *Only Murders in the Building* (which I do watch and enjoy). This show has the perfect balance of amateur programming a.k.a. podcasting, murder, and self-admiration wrapped in a whodunnit. Our society programs, promotes, sleuths and speculates with sometimes good judgement and often times a lack thereof. The *Building* trio breaks all kinds of rules with regards to crime scenes, evidence and investigation. It's a comedy. Murder is simply a vehicle wrapping the ensemble into a whirlwind of zaniness. *Alfred Hitchcock Presents* similarly used the host's droll campy introductions to delight us with the murderous tale being presented—a way of balancing dark and light in a period when graphic violence wasn't depicted. The difference today is our world feeds on killer stories. True crime documentaries, scripted biopics, episodic of anything from horror to suspense to video games that include masterfully explicit special effects that may or may not be realistic and could inspire the wrong people. Do we really wonder why crime is a problem? We blame access to guns, but what fuels the need to own one? What fuels the need to use one? Please don't confuse any of this with support for guns. I hate guns. It can't be healthy to come home from a stressful or unfulfilling job to binge on shows focused on how to commit a crime and possibly get away with it. I'm not a mental health professional, but common sense would dictate everything in moderation. Right? Moderation in, shouldn't we put the brakes on violent content?

And lost in the majority of crime dramas are the victims. Unless the murdered are famous, the murderer will take the spotlight. As sick as saying spotlight is, the criminal, God help me for saying this, is the showrunner. The murderer becomes famous. How many of us remember one victim name of a serial killing? Victims are income generators for the murder genre revenue machine. The where, when, why, and how of their deaths are treated as plot points and the victim a game piece to be moved around a crime scene.

And I do understand that well-meaning true crime podcasters and amateur sleuths want to help solve cold cases, but could a show's popularity skew the host and crew's thinking to become more competitive with their fellow podcasters and lose sight of people who lost their lives? Might someone be wrongly accused or targeted by a host's or crew's blind ambition? If a crime is solved with the help of non-traditional investigators, could it amp-up more wannabes whose intentions are sincere but skills are questionable? Do victims' families have a say and involvement in how their loved one is portrayed, given the dead can't speak for themselves? Other than perhaps *America's Most Wanted*; do true crime activists seek the public's help for tips? Where does law enforcement stand on the self-deputized detective?

I'm getting to a point about writing true crime, trust me. The best example of unconventional crime solving would be author Michelle McNamara's brilliant nonfiction case, *I'll Be Gone in the Dark: One Woman's Obsessive Search for the Golden State Killer* that aided law enforcement (through DNA analysis aided by Barbara Rae-Venter, see her book *I Know Who You Are: How an Amateur DNA Sleuth Unmasked the Golden State Killer And Changed Crime Fighting Forever*) in finding and ultimately arresting the Golden State Killer after McNamara's unexpected death. The HBO documentary of McNamara's writing process, the clues, the findings, and the toll it took on her quality of life and ultimately the author's sudden death are scary. Her sacrifice brought justice for the victims and their families, but her fixation ultimately took her life it would seem. Her exhaustive determination made her another victim of murderer Joseph James DeAngelo.

Journalist Tom O'Neill's *Chaos: Charles Manson, the CIA, and the Secret History of the Sixties* began as an article to expose more details of the Manson family murders of Sharon Tate, her eight-month-old unborn son Paul Polanski, Jay Sebring, Abigail Folger, Wojciech Frykowski, Steven Parent, and an additional couple

Leno and Rosemary LaBianca. O'Neill with similar resolve wasn't trying to find a killer but uncover government conspiracy, law enforcement failures, as well as get answers from a tightlipped list of Hollywood celebrities who knew more than they were willing to divulge. His article morphed into a book that took a financial and physical toll on his wellbeing. Over twenty years he continued to find evidence, interview people and finally he and Dan Piepenbring organized his research into a finished product. So, what do we do with this data?

In the story I'm sharing, I'm not including names or specific locations. I have not consulted the victims' families, and I have no desire to promote murderers. I'm simply speaking of what was my teenage mindset in hopes that it gives someone peace of mind or an understanding they might be seeking.

Like most teens, I didn't want parental discipline and boundaries at times. I accepted them and stretched them once I started working at fourteen. I was very naïve when I became acquainted with older teenagers who took risks. My mother trusted me. There was no reason not to. I hadn't done anything to cause her concern. She wasn't aware that my blinders were off, that my field of vision had dramatically increased. I was a quiet kid who watched and wondered. No one harmed or bullied me into doing anything. I tried things to try things. I wasn't escaping reality or some inner pain. I was having a go at things the same as riding a bicycle, hammering a nail, or walking to the store alone.

My brothers and I were part-timers at a local carwash. Funds were limited when our parents divorced. The carwash job provided us with spending money, and me with an income. Our dad wasn't a deadbeat, he paid the agreed upon child support and even mortgage payments, but it wasn't enough at times for our household of five. As mentioned in the opening chapter, I was in a Work

The Murderer

Experience program starting in junior high. By working, we (my siblings and I) were able to buy our own clothes, pay for movies and fast food, and give Mom money for milk if needed. I even began to pay for my own dental bills. My mother walked with me to the dentist, got all the paperwork started as the parent, then I began the patient relationship. I had regular appointments. I walked to the dentist. The dentist would lecture me on my poor dental hygiene, fill my cavities, and set the next appointment which was about $40 a visit.

But I didn't go to work to pay for my fillings. I wanted to work. I liked being productive, meeting and watching intriguing people. Lots of expensive cars rolled in from Belleair, wealthy people, women who had pitchers of mimosas they carried into our waiting area. They poured themselves drinks while waiting for their car. Elegant ladies who complained about the pain of tummy tucks, the price of facials, and the travel that was delayed because their executive husbands had to work. They had kids my age and older who were graduating high school and applying for college or traveling abroad. Rich kids who were gifted a Datsun 240Z, Trans Am, Mustang or a hand-me-down Mercedes SL series as their first car. The Belleair wives were movie star gorgeous and tipped decently. Oftentimes they traveled in trios or foursomes to Sarasota or Sanibel Island for a fundraiser or luncheon priority in one of their freshly washed Lincoln Continentals, Cadillacs or Bentleys. They didn't need air fresheners for their cars. They wore enough perfume to make the interior smell like a bouquet of flowers. Then there were the police cars and attorney's Mercedes, and of course trashed family station wagons. Patrons came from all social classes. The retirees encouraged us to go to college, talked longer than they needed to. Real estate agents and the average mom wanted to get in and out quickly. They had places to be.

Pimps and drug dealers were pointed out by my coworkers, never as a warning, just, he's a pimp. He's a drug dealer. Pimps and drug dealers drove older model Cadillacs with wide white wall tires. They weren't interested in small talk, either. I didn't question any of these labels. I just observed and did my job. Most customers were nice, some accused us of scratching their car, or a gun would go missing from a lawyer's car and the extra change from a cup holder. God forbid an antenna would snap. Scratches were the higher drama. Employees couldn't wear belts or have keys dangling from a belt loop as a result.

The car wash also employed older workers, too. Older to me was in anyone over 30. This was a 1970s mom-and-pop business which closed for a half-hour lunch break daily to give us enough time to jog to a nearby Burger Chef or KFC (four to five blocks away before drive throughs were the norm) to wait in line for our order and gulp our food running back. Driving to a fast-food restaurant wasn't speedier. You still had to stand in line and wait for your order, then maneuver small parking lots that were jammed with cars backing out, pulling in, or occupying two spaces. I still eat too fast.

At this time, I became good friends with a coworker who was sixteen. She was an only child and owned a 1965 Ford Galaxy (I believe) thanks to her considerate blue-collar parents. Up to this point, I had no idea the size of our city beyond where my feet could take me or the cab fare my mother could afford (which was a couple of mile radius). My friend opened my horizons to a county of multiple cities. With my mother's permission I could go with my friend as far as her gas tank would take us. Actually, my mother didn't think we'd go anywhere other than where we said we were going. At that time, gas was under .50 cents a gallon and we made about $1.25 an hour. If I chipped in, the possibilities seemed endless.

The Murderer

Our first weekend adventure, we headed to north county. We found a small town with a group of mostly immature young guys who hung out in front of a convenience store with a couple of teenage girls. They all seemed bored. Since my friend was their age, she engaged in conversation with them. I observed. We barely registered consideration. They ignored us. We were nobody.

These loiters' first order of business was to obtain cigarettes, then find someone who would buy them beer. Cigarettes were under .50 cents a pack and plentiful. Someone always bought them beer.

In the beginning, our weekend escapades were to places completely unknown to me. I would let my mother know when I was home and off to bed I went. She didn't put me on a curfew. My mother, I'm assuming, seemed to expect my friend's parents would limit the hours she could drive. Thus, we'd have a curfew. I came home smelling of cigarettes. My mother seemed to accept I'd eventually try smoking. Our dad smoked. It wasn't like she approved but seemed to be observing without lecturing. Maybe choosing her battles.

Since my friend's car was a larger vehicle, we would become transportation for the convenience store strays who wanted transportation to the beach, their parent's home, or sometimes a vacant lot where bonfires commenced. The guys were mostly interested in building and stoking the fire or getting high. The girls were interested in making out with whatever guy they were interested in. I was interested in one guy who wasn't really interested in making out with me. We made out a few times. He tolerated my groupie behavior but that was it. No one tried to force themselves on us. We were the girls who showed up on Friday or Saturday and sometimes paid for their cigarettes.

It was also well known amongst these guys that statutory rape was real. A term I learned from them. In their definition, a guy could have sex with his underage girlfriend up to eighteen. After a guy turned eighteen, any girl under eighteen was off limits, even if that girl had been his girlfriend his whole life—because now her parents could have him arrested and hauled to jail for having intercourse with a minor equaling statutory rape. By this point I had already seen movies like *The Summer of '42* and *The Prime of Miss Jean Brody*. Movies that showed inappropriate relationships of teens or students with adults versus relationships among a peer group. So, I can't say I even rationalized these sex theories or the legality. I heard all kinds of stuff at the carwash, too. To me, our weekend adventures weren't dangerous, other than drinking. I knew we were underage.

None of my activities would have happened if my parents had stayed together. My parents would not have let us work or would have only allowed my older brother to work jobs deemed safe and suitable as they related to his ability to keep up with schoolwork. Drugs back then were speed and pot. The carwash family employed drug dealers unknowingly. Some were the rich kids from Belleair who dealt pot. I tried pot, got heart palpitations and didn't like it. When I tried Boone's Farm and Mad Dog 20/20 (Mogen David 20/20) sweet wines, I liked them. Oddly, I had a tolerance that seemed unlikely for someone who had never even sipped alcohol prior. In the early 1970s drinking and driving were not against the law. It was to be avoided. Mobile parties were commonplace. Teens followed the grown-ups example.

When we finished work on Friday afternoons, we'd cash our paychecks, head to Sunshine Mall's Stuarts clothing store and buy a new outfit, grab McDonald's for dinner or eat with our family, then head to north county.

Our first encounter with the murderer (he hadn't murdered yet), was at the convenience store. I'll call him Dare Devil or DD.

He was excitable, dorky, definitely not a jock but a class clown type who owned a motorcycle. He would perform any stunt dared. He thrived on crowd approval. The most impressive was driving at top speed standing on his motorcycle seat with arms outstretched. This happened at dark. He flew down the two-lane highway on muscle memory. Today he might be considered an extreme sports type. He had no fear. Exhilaration equaled delirium. He craved attention and dare requests. He wasn't very articulate, maybe learning disabled. He'd jump into a canal, orange bomb cars (throw mushy rotten oranges at cars), lift hundreds of pounds of unanchored weights, and backwards motorcycle stunts. We thought he was hilarious. He wasn't bullied. He sought dangerous challenges. Back then, the only entertainer who was doing motorcycle feats was stunt performer, Evel Knievel. He was televised jumping a line of cars in Las Vegas and often times he broke lots of bones when unsuccessful. Knievel was one of a kind. X-Games didn't exist. Not that we even knew if DD watched Knievel, it's just a reference point for the time.

Dare Devil's calm, brooding moments were often followed by maniacal giggling. To his friends, he was just part of the group. To outsiders, he was a bit crazy. One moonless night several in the crowd wanted to go to a nearby beach to stargaze and drink. DD joined us in my friend's car instead of driving his motorcyle. He was really quiet, possibly upset. As the moon stayed hidden behind dark clouds, we walked in pairs. I walked fast beside him, barefoot. He wore shoes and walked heavily like someone tasked with crushing seashells versus strolling. Many tried to light cigarettes though it was too windy. I was cold and my bare feet were killing me. We didn't stay. It was too windy. On the walk back to the car, I discovered that most of what I was walking on was broken shells and glass. It seemed this stretch of beach was a party spot and as such bottles got broken there often. I left bloody footprints along our path. This would be our last contact.

Shortly thereafter, for reasons that weren't revealed to me, my friend was grounded and stopped working at the carwash. I was actually glad our activities and travels stopped. Our routine was getting boring. We were becoming as apathetic as the convenience store crowd, an expansion group sitting in a vehicle while they stood outside the store. Creatures of monotony. I wouldn't see my friend again for a few years.

Fast forward, at seventeen, I saw a newspaper article in the *Clearwater Sun* newspaper, the paper for which I would later write. The story was about a couple of teens who were murdered on the same beach where I cut my feet. Their killer(s) still on the loose. Subsequent stories were released and a pair of murder suspects apprehended. To my shock, one of the two apprehended was Dare Devil. His partner in the crime was a criminal with priors. I felt sick. The victims were sixteen and seventeen. I was younger when I left my bloody prints on the same beach I'd walked with DD, fortunate to walk away. The victims had been out to enjoy a sunset and never had a chance to go home. It was reported that the couple and perpetrators were neighbors and lived close proximity. They knew each other. Reading the article, I was certain DD was the accomplice and his partner the one who plotted the murder. It seemed plausible. I clipped articles and tried to stay up on the case and the trial. Eventually both were convicted in separate trials that had twists.

After several more years passed, when I was studying journalism and wrote the first draft of this story, I thought I might want to write a book. I called the detective who worked on the case, he was now a police captain, very helpful and wanted to know where my story would be published. I was honest, I didn't know. I was

The Murderer

> I called the detective who worked on the case, he was now a police captain, very helpful and wanted to know where my story would be published. I was honest, I didn't know.

starting the process. I was still a student. He listened and said I could come by and we'd talk. I told him my story, how I knew one of the criminals. He pulled the case and asked me if I was going to be okay looking at the crime scene photos. I said I thought I would be. I sought the officer's advice regarding several people I wanted to interview. One individual had been a primary suspect that I learned had a sexual assault history. Captain didn't think it was a good idea for me to pursue that interview. He also told me of several challenges they had in the investigation. Things that didn't appear in news articles. Things I'd write about if I were telling the whole story. I spent an evening reviewing the case file. I felt dirty examining the photos.

Why was I doing this? How would the families feel about me dredging this up again? Couldn't the victims just rest in peace? Was I an opportunist? How would this honor the victims? Did I have a point or was I just going to boast that I knew one of these criminals? I wasn't sure.

Two points stood out: (1) my friend and I took risks. We lived. (2) The victims were just out to watch the sunset. They're dead.

If I had died on a freewheeling weekend, it would have been considered uncharacteristic for me. Friends and family would have said there was no way I went to a city so far from my home. I was a quiet girl, a good Catholic girl, a hardworking girl who helped her mother. And all of those statements would be true. But I was also testing teenage boundaries, coming of age, underage. We weren't pushed to do anything. There was no pressure on my friend and me. We were simply good kids misbehaving. At times we sat around, it wasn't always a party. We didn't have smart phones to distract us or to capture evidence of our activities or track our whereabouts.

And since I lived to grow up, get married, have children, and a future, I include this to caution people from daring others to do dangerous things as we don't know how it influences the risk-taker and the potential ripple effect. Someone is likely to get hurt. I'm not implying they'll become a killer. Some risktakers become brilliant scientists, athletes, artists and entrepreneurs. I'm not a mental health professional, but since I was acquainted with someone risk motivated, I'm prone to believe it contributed to his role in assault and murder. And moreover, to all parents, follow your gut instincts, rein in your children, especially the quiet ones (not that all quiet children are gullible), but they could be capable of straying. That's the part that haunts me still. If I met Charles Manson or Ted Bundy and they were polite, not creepy in my presence, would I have followed them?

Samuel Shere,
Real Estate Investor &
Life Magazine Photographer

Real Estate photo by Samuel Shere

I met Samuel Shere across a closing table at G.W. Stone Realtor office in St. Petersburg, Fl., June 14, 1977. I didn't know who he was, other than the seller of a piece of real estate I was about to purchase. My mother was with me. She talked to Shere about his storied photography career. Neither Mom nor I knew the name Samuel Shere before that day. When he mentioned photographing the Duke and Duchess of Windsor while Adela Rogers St. John was reporting on the event, my mother chimed in that she had just read Rogers, *Final Verdict*. He appreciated that my Mom could hold her own in a conversation about his connections. They continued dishing about notable people. My mother, the ultimate magazine reader, knew Shere was important. Famous! Because he photographed historic events and renowned people for *Life Magazine*.

The little house, as I called it, in South St. Petersburg was my first real estate acquisition. Not that there were many. The picture above was photographed by Shere. My mother discovered the ad for (a house and unfinished building behind the main house) for the asking price of $9,750. Both buildings could be purchased for a small down payment and the seller would hold the mortgage. *A small down payment* captured my mother's attention. The home already had tenants, so there was little risk. The second building could be converted into an efficiency, but I never had the resources to do anything. The tenants used it for storage. Having no credit or available cash herself, my mother brought the idea to me. I was reluctant to consider it. I had enough savings for the $150 down to sign the contract and there would be $1100 more due at closing which would use up most of my savings. However, my mother was certain that I could sell it and make a decent profit when the time came. At eighteen, just about to turn nineteen my achievements were: I finished night school, got my high school diploma, worked full time, saved money, and traveled alone for the first time (ever) to Canada. The trip was a month before May 1977. My round-trip ticket on Air Canada was $213.13. I went to Ontario to visit my neighbor's college student nephew. I only needed a U.S. driver's license, as I didn't have a passport. By my mother's interpretation, I was a world traveler. There was nothing I couldn't do. I agreed, but my goal was to travel and write, not necessarily landlord.

Samuel Shere, Real Estate Investor & Life Magazine Photographer

I sat at the closing not sure what to focus on, listening to my mother and Shere go over his photo captures: the Hindenburg explosion and more. It was apparent to me that Shere was the most important person in the room, though everyone treated me like I was. They were counting on me to make the transaction happen. I provided the downpayment, signed all the papers, promising to pay Shere $83.71 on the 14th of every month for the mortgage he held of $8500. My annual gross income in those days was about $9,000. I lived at home and helped my mother pay bills, as well I paid car payments, car repairs, and auto insurance.

Once the real estate transaction was done, I signed a rental agreement designating me as the new property owner for the tenants, an elderly African American couple, who would now pay me a monthly rent of $125.00 of which $34 cash was out of their pocket and $91 a month would be mailed directly to me from their H.U.D (Housing and Urban Development) assistance. I would bank $41.29 monthly that I put aside for repairs, homeowner's insurance and if at some point there was something leftover, I might make a profit.

It all started out great. I would get a check in the mail and pick up the tenant's cash at times or they'd mail me a money order. The tenants were good people and kept the house neat, lawn mowed and were happy to continue to live in an affordable place. Shere's check was timed for the 14th of the month, my tenants rent was perhaps a week earlier than my mortgage payments. The challenge came in the timing of deposits and mailing checks to Shere.

If my check didn't reach him on the fourteenth of the month, he sent me a letter saying that defaulting on a payment would lead to foreclosure. I wish I had saved at least one of those letters. They really upset me. It was embarrassing getting foreclosure warnings. For Shere, the letter was an instrument to keep his mortgagor on notice, a natural course of action for a mortgage holder. He was an investor and likely had multiple Emilys he sent these letters to. I was a neurotically serious nineteen-year-old with trust issues. Serious as far as anything legal was concerned. He was an authority figure. Could I go to jail for foreclosure? I was not mature enough to understand that he couldn't foreclose that easily. Shere lived on the other coast of Florida and didn't have a phone. He relied on the mail for his payments and correspondence. Would I lose all of the money I had paid him because I was a few days late paying? Could my lateness be compounded?

Then there was my land lording occupation—which I felt was a punishment vs. my introduction into the world of private enterprise. As a full-time car washer and later detailer at a Saab and Subaru dealership, I didn't know I was an entrepreneur. I hadn't even heard the term until years later. While everyone was impressed that I was an investor, I was certain it was some kind of a cruel joke. There was nothing impressive about being totally inexperienced at procuring quality home improvements for the little house. My poor tenants endured my changing out their four-burner gas stove with an antique two-burner gas stove because it was all I could afford. But I replaced their stove. My brother installed it, they called the gas company (because they could tell we didn't know much) to have it properly installed, for which I reimbursed them. I was saving less, and suddenly everything was breaking down everywhere. I was overwhelmed by my tenants, my actual employer, my family and Shere. About six months or so into ownership I completely freaked out and drove to New Smyrna Beach where Shere lived to deliver my late mortgage payment in person. I was convinced I was going to get arrested.

My mother and I drove over to see Shere at his apartment and he happily received us. Actually, he was delighted to see my mother.

She was a captive audience for him. His apartment's living room was filled with cameras and memorabilia and he was more than happy to share their backstory. I was confused. As I gave him his check and explained how worried I was about his foreclosure letters, he seemed to understand and served us refreshments and talked more about his life. My mother loved his story about covering the Duke and Duchess of Windsor. He told us (well, her) that the Duke and former king helped him with the lighting for a photo he took of the Duke's wife, the Duchess of Windsor, the former Wallis Simpson. My mother couldn't get enough. He talked about working undercover in Sing Sing prison. Funny how prison fears and prison stories were the topic of that day. You'd think I would have been relieved, but I was completely puzzled. I drove there like I was trying to stop a bomb from going off and was greeted by a nice man who loved visitors and talking about himself. The foreclosure warnings didn't stop after the visit. He continued his practice if the check didn't arrive on the 14th. Some notifications came from his son when Shere was traveling. I endured entrepreneurship but did not enjoy it.

The next year I convinced my mother to sell the home we lived in. The house needed too many repairs and rodents were becoming a problem. I took out a loan from a finance company to have the house carpeted with blue shag and I painted most of the interior myself in baby blue to make it look new. Funny, I became better at handling things related to my family's home, than my tenants. My Dad technically owned the house. He was responsible for that mortgage in their divorce settlement. With my father's blessing, he allowed my mother to keep the earnings from the sale of the house to buy another. He would no longer be responsible. We sold the house to the first person who looked. And since Mom had no credit, we got a joint FHA (Federal Housing Administration) loan to buy another home. I would become an owner again with her because I had a job and credit. This would be the home where my mother, my sister, my younger brother and myself, would reside.

Now I had two mortgages and my mother had money in the bank to pay for the payments and some remodeling in the first year. I never considered either house mine. I thought of the investment property as my tenant's home and my mother's home as the place where my immediate family lived. I was happy to be able to provide, but I was becoming financially overwhelmed. I worked two and three jobs at times. My dream of becoming a journalist was moving further away.

I owned the little house for three and a half years and paid Shere every month, roughly a total of $3515.82. I sold the house for $2000 above my remaining loan obligation in December of 1980. Shere got his mortgage paid off and I made $2000, which helped pay me off other debts I owed. I was done being a landlord. I still owned a home with my mother but was ready to focus on college courses and writing. Shere was happy. I finally felt comfortable enough to ask if I could interview him. Would he photograph my family? He was agreeable to both, but neither happened. Our last communication came about eight months after I sold the little house.

To summarize his background as provided from the article by Joanne Kash in *Art Voices South*.

He was born Samuel Shereshewsky in Minsk, Russia 1905. Minsk is in Belarus, a Soviet territory. His father shortened their last name when the family immigrated to New York. To his father's disappointment, Sam quit school after seventh grade to become a $1-a-day tripod caddy for Pathe New Cameramen. Understanding his son's sincere interest in a photography career, his father would eventually buy him a 4x5 Speed Graphic camera that provided Sam the ability to sell his own work to news agencies.

1/1/81

Dear Miss Williams,

I was glad your house finally sold and hoped you realize some profit. The check came just in time for me as I was in the hospital for 9 days.

Enclosed is my only copy of the Dec '80 issue of "Art Voices South" published in W. Palm Beach and goes to 22 states. Originally the interview was made 2 years ago and I was born in 1905 instead of '04 in Russia.

You might want to Zerox the story possibly your college might be interested in my exhibit and talk once I get back from New York where I call on LIFE and U.P.I. for a selection of my best historic pictures. I am scheduled to be at Western Carolina University N.C. in February.

Take your picture... sure if I get to St. Pete, also your family.

Do return my tear sheet story. The Magazine sells for $2.75 plus $1.00 postage and is issued every 2 months. My story was in Nov. Dec. '80. It is a very high class magazine and the address is ART VOICES Publishing, Co., 324 Datura St., W. Palm Beach, 33401

Happy New Year to you all.

Samuel Shere

In 1925 Shere purchased a Leica 35mm camera in Germany. He used both cameras, the larger 4x5 Speed Graphic and the smaller, lighter Leica which he snuck into the courtroom to take photos of Lindbergh kidnapping suspect Bruno Richard

Hauptmann who was later convicted of the kidnapping and murder of Charles Lindbergh, Jr. He shared some of these stories the day we visited him in New Smyrna, but I was so overwhelmed that it took reading the article to realize I had heard him telling my mother these same memories.

Shere was also a ship's photographer and made 126 crossings. He traveled with Eleanor Roosevelt during the Roosevelt campaign and photographed crime scenes, breaking news as it happened, among a litany of society events, celebrities, politicians, criminals, world leaders, even the average citizen. In retirement he boasted of enjoying travel, lecturing, and real estate investing. He was frugal by all indications and died in 1982 I discovered from online sources. Knowing I had last communicated with him in 1981, I feel fortunate to have sold the little house and closed that chapter peacefully.

His last letter came in August of 1981.

8/5/81

Dear Emily,

Recently returned from Tiger, Ga, Rabun County and was glad to hear from you. Enclosed is a copy of *The Pelican* which went to 3 newspapers, copy it and return no hurry. I still lecture at Daytona Beach Community College photography dept. I may go to Ireland this Fall to do a picture story in which the Irish Tourist Bureau in New York is interested in. In April a reporter for the Munich Germany magazine interviewed me on my Hindenburg pictures. The issue is due soon. You may interview me anytime I am in New Smyrna, I have no phone after 40 years (not 30) as the enclosed story mentions a phone was always on me, so I am happy to be without one. My best regards to you and your Mother.

    Cordially,
    Samuel Shere

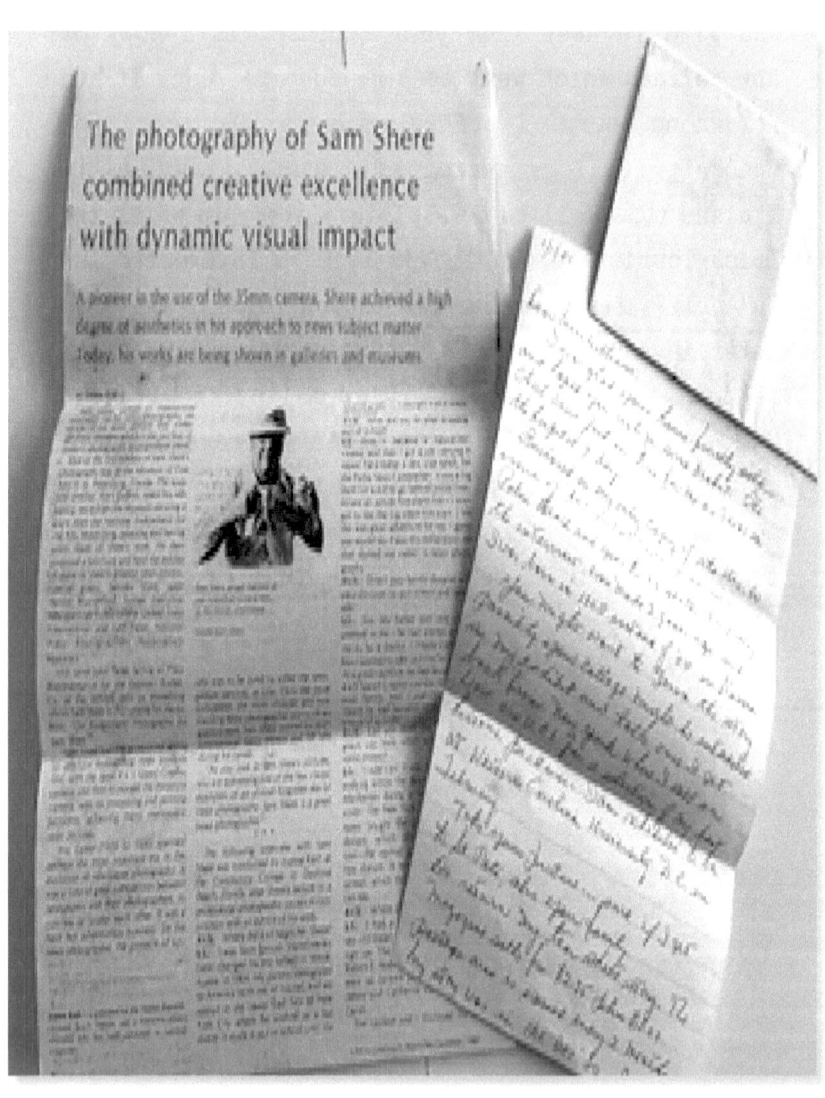

All photos of letters and personal effects by Emily W. Skinner

Samuel Shere, Real Estate Investor & Life Magazine Photographer

All photos of letters and personal effects by Emily W. Skinner

Bono-mania

At 29 I was obsessed with Bono, U2's *Joshua Tree* tour, and not turning 30. I had even started writing a Harlequin Romance about a woman who meets a celebrated Irish musician at a concert in Tampa. Which brings me to my Richard Harris obsession, after seeing *Man in the Wilderness*, I started writing an Irish romance about an underage girl marrying a Harris-like widower to care for his child. The Irish roots conjure. But I'm getting ahead of myself.

December 5, 1987, I experienced U2's *Joshua Tree* tour concert at the Old Sombrero, the former Tampa Bay Bucs football stadium. Buckwheat Zydeco and Los Lobos opened. Now keep in mind "opening act" is important to this story.

My then 18-year-old sister, Ellen, a true confidante and support when it comes to all things unrealistic and unreasonable was very consoling prior to my 30th birthday. She indulged my fantasy to meet Bono and ditch the husband and kid to live on the road with the Irish hunk. I equally indulged her quest to stalk Don Henley of the Eagles when she was in need. This was after her Steve Perry / Journey obsession. However, she was a better stalker (in the most innocent groupie way) than I am finder of superstar musicians.

Anyway, Ellen and my then sister-in-law, Linda (very pregnant with my niece) managed to take an escalator ride with Henley and a traveling companion at Tampa airport when he was in town for his solo *The End of The Innocence* tour. We published an article about the happening in my zine *Bohemian Chronicle* (See Bohemian Chronicle chapter*)*. Ellen was really good at wooing band staff for details of said artist's whereabouts. I guess it's a family trait (see Hank Williams, Jr.) but I don't possess Ellen's eloquence. Shh! She doesn't want you to know she wrote an amazing 600+ page novel about a woman who joins a rock band and rises to stardom, because she's weird about becoming famous herself. Go figure! To clarify, Ellen received the only significant praise of our writer's pact having achieved a *St. Petersburg Times* review of her self-published novel, (she doesn't want me to share the title) when the iUniverse was just beginning. iUniverse was the printing entity we both self-published with before many more companies joined the trend and surpassed them, notably, Amazon. Anyway, *The Times* nixed reviewing self-published authors almost immediately after my sister's review was discovered among their literary endorsements. It seems *The Times* had some sort of standards to maintain. Bravo to my renegade sister! She deserves accolades, though there was nothing rebel about submitting a book for review. It was the maverick reviewer that slipped the praise past her senior editor. Though, if Ellen's rock saga had not been worthy, it would not have happened. I've been jealous ever since, but equally proud.

Moving on. In 1989 (see Harry Whittington) I wrote my first novel, *Marquel* in longhand. U2's *I Still Haven't Found What I'm Looking For* stuck in my head as a theme while writing the book. The drama screened as movie before me as I followed a detailed outline. This story needed a theatrical release, I was convinced. And once again, I sought my sister's sympathy for Bono love. She edited *Marquel*. Now, mind you, Bono didn't appear in the *Marquel* novel. His music fueled the writing. (P.S.) Kevin Costner was a character fixation for my George Jennings. I saw Costner play charity baseball in St. Petersburg. That's not part of the Bono story. Stay with me. Ellen understood Bono-mania. By the way, if you know Bono, or if he ever receives word of this, I still need *ISHFWILF* for the film's opening sequence when I finally secure a backer for the movie version. I have written the screenplay if he wants to read it. Sorry for the interruption.

In case I've lost you:

- Bono
- *Joshua Tree*
- *Say No To 30!*
- *My stalker sister*
- *My novel Marquel*
- *I Still Haven't Found What I'm Looking For*
- Return of Bono-mania

So, I'm whining to Ellen about Bono providing me rights to his music for a future film and Ellen said, "You should have said something when you met him."

"What!?"

My sister is clearly a smart ass. I wouldn't have ignored Bono if I had met him.

"When you were at the J. Geils concert. They opened for J. Geils."

Like one of those movie pull-in shots, where the actor is standing or sitting there and all of a sudden, the camera zooms in to the person's realization. Think Roy Scheider in *Jaws*.

"What are you talking about?"

She does this sing-songy explanation of how I went to the J. Geils concert and U2 opened for J. Geils, and how I had bragged that I went to the after event the radio station was hosting. Then she doubles down on "The band was there."

I'm partially paralyzed at this point.

"Wait?!" I am thinking.

Flashback: I'm at the Curtis Hixon Hall in Tampa, Friday March 5, 1982. J. Geils has concluded the evening's *Centerfold* concert performance. I'm with a photographer from *Steppin Out* local entertainment guide, one of my freelance trades. Meaning, I go to events free and write reviews. Anyway, we are offered a chance to meet lead singer Peter Wolf (aka Faye Dunaway's ex-husband)

Article photo by Emily W. Skinner

and the J. Geils band. I'm drawing a complete blank on the opening act. Did we get there for the opening act? Did we ignore the opening act?

Ellen sees my puzzled expression. She adds, "They were at the after party."

More flashback: I'm walking into a small white room with the photographer. There are some refreshments and a lot of small pale men with long dark hair looking lost. Everyone is quiet. A local DJ comes in and says something loud and obnoxious. People laugh.

It hits me.

"Oh my God!" *I was in the same room with Bono!*

Do you want to know what happened in that room?

Absolutely nothing. Everyone stood around waiting for someone to start mingling. All the musicians seemed like flat vinyl *Colorform* dolls, but not colorful. Very anemic. I wasn't sure who was who and besides we were going to breakfast after. I'm very food driven, so that's distracting.

We hung around a few minutes and left. The photographer published great photos of J. Geils Band. I wrote an oddball review. There were no U2 photos, so I've deduced that we missed the opening act. At times I still try to see the after party in my mind's eye and they're just cartoon stick figures. *Damn it!*

Blow Me a Kiss, Paul!

My Paul McCartney obsession began at six-years-old. Like my character Everly Knight in *The Movie Queen*, I am a Beatles fan and as such, I believed I would grow up to marry my Beatle—because dreams really do come true. I recommend you purchase *The Movie Queen*.

In 2019 I discovered that Paul McCartney would be playing at Dodgers Stadium on my birthday. A sign from God! Our daughters lived in Los Angeles at the time and having never really splurged on a bucket list item, I bought tickets for my husband, Tom, and myself. I had secretly hoped my family would buy tickets and surprise me, but once I had shared the news that McCartney would be performing on my birthday it was met with, "That's cool." I knew hinting was useless.

My first husband, Paul McCartney, well, that was the plan when I was six… had expensive ticket packages that promised good seats and merch. We received McCartney totes, luggage tags, commemorative tickets, beach towels, and a compact disc of his latest album. My friend Kim Salter is a concert savant and as such buys all kinds of tickets that include meet and greets. If Paul had offered a meet and greet and there was a chance for a speedy divorce from Tom—and Mary McCartney cooperated, Paul and I would be together today. Anyway, if there was a meet and greet at Dodger's Stadium, don't tell me! I already missed my chance with Bono…

Anyhow, the seats weren't as close as I imagined they would be, but the jumbo screens made up for proximity. All of the material goods were appreciated but don't hold a candle to what happened. Okay, you're going to say he didn't do this for me alone, but I believe in my constitutional right to the pursuit of happiness.

Back to it. I wore my Cavern Club t-shirt I got in Liverpool the year before and my husband wore a random plain t-shirt, unlike him. He's a very thoughtful dresser, but sweats easily and perhaps he strategically wore this to hide perspiration. Nevertheless, as soon as we got there, I was giddy. Beyond giddy. I immediately noticed the TEXT ME sign Paul's people had thoughtfully placed there (for me). I instantly texted as evidenced below. My phone was on East Coast time as it reads 10:01 pm, and it was 7:01 pm in California. "Hi Paul! I'm in row 43FD row b, seat 7. Blow me kisses!! It's my birthday!! @emilyauthor Instagram."

I won't recount the magical mystery tour of songs that Sir Paul played. I took pictures and videos throughout the night and soon forgot my text to Paul as Ringo and Joe Walsh made surprise appearances. As the concert concluded, with encores completed, the band had left the stage. Swooning and in a state of euphoria, I was divinely inspired to bring my camera back up and point it toward the stage. A hurried Paul reappeared to blow a kiss and left. OH MY GOD! How did I capture this? It was my kiss. MY KISS! My text request. OH MY GOD! Happy birthday to me! Thank you so much universe, Jesus and maybe John Lennon and George Harrison who worked a heavenly miracle to inspire me to take a photo of the unexpected. Story evidence is so much better than a story without—as you'll see in the Cesar Romero interview.

If you are asking yourself why this self-indulgent woman is boasting and bragging about something she perceived happened.

Because it did happen! The end.

Blow me a kiss, Paul!

Photo of Tom and Emily Skinner by a concert goer using Emily W. Skinner's phone

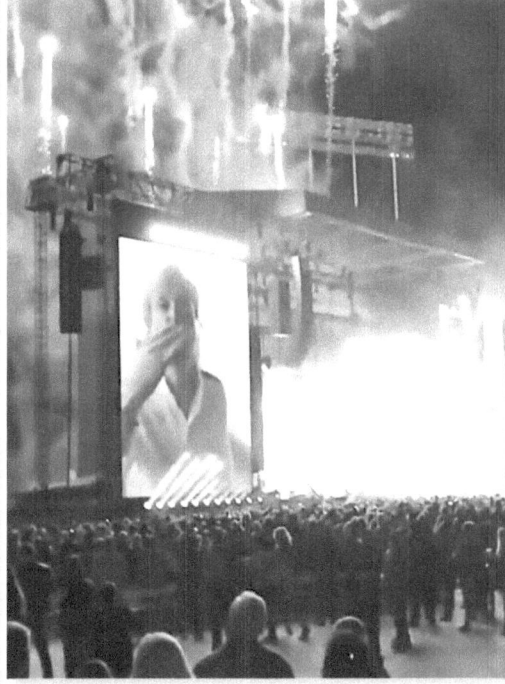

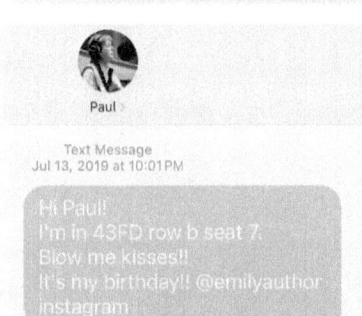

Three remaining Photos by Emily W. Skinner

Cesar Romero, Picture This!

My Collection of Cesar Romero Programs & Articles. Photo by Emily W. Skinner

I saw Cesar Romero at our local dinner theater five of the six times he performed. To my generation, he was The Joker on television's *Batman*. I wasn't attracted to The Joker. I learned from a trivia game he wore white makeup over his moustache when he played the villain. He was never without a moustache it seems and wouldn't shave it. I can't imagine seeing Romero playing the Joker without makeup. That's actually frightening. The Joker was a fun character; a mildly insane Cesar Romero would not be. I was probably his youngest groupie among the dinner theatre's collective of dressed-up buffet eaters. I considered marrying him. These were thoughts I pondered while single. There was something mesmerizing about his commanding presence and ageless masculinity. It wasn't a father or grandfather complex. Although, I'm not knowledgeable enough in psychology to debate the point. It wasn't his old films, as I didn't see many. But instead, it was the way he carried himself and talked to his audience after the performance. He treated the entire room like welcomed guests at his hacienda. We were his big happy family. When he took questions, he looked you in the eye. Gave you that Dracula smile. Come to think of it, he could've played Dracula. He had the stature of Christopher Lee or Frank Langella. He was a leading man in the tradition of my mother's lifelong crush, Clark Gable. Mom indoctrinated me into viewing older men as pleasant suitors over silly boys my own age. She judged men for their charisma and height, as in tall, dark and handsome. You see my mother always considered graying at the temples a distinguished look. Not that I dated senior citizens. To her, Cesar Romero was an uncommonly charming relic of Hollywood's Golden Age with notable ancestry to boot, and as such, his thick white hair was well rooted in a tan Cuban scalp that did not show a hint of balding. Rare indeed. We (Mom and I) didn't see age in the debonaire 6' 3" giant, though I admit I have since found gray or white hair unattractive. Sorry to all silvern men for any harm inflicted. To be clear, Mom was divorced at the time (she never stopped loving my father) and she wanted me to consider the possibilities of a star-man. She never said star-man, I just combined the star and his gender. I think she wanted to see her family on pages of her favorite movie magazines. A guesstimate of the number of Hollywood gossip magazines Mom bought in her adulthood could realistically be set at 3,120 on the low side, figuring 52 weeks at one magazine a week up to age 78. She rarely bought only one. A gallon of milk and two magazines were staples in our house (provided there was Hershey's chocolate syrup at home for the milk), otherwise the syrup replaced one magazine. Once Mom became less mobile, she relied on subscriptions. Her multiple subscriptions brought the total to 10,000 magazines easily.

Where were we?

Somewhere along the way, I secured an interview with the Latin from Manhattan. A pattern you'll see throughout these pages. I'd secure an interview before I had an assignment or tried to sell a spec article after an interview, or cluelessly get insecure and procrastinate forty years and finally put them into a memoir.

The Cesar Romero query letter earned a request for a spec article from a national publication that catered to senior citizens. I'd assumed the Romero interview when I mailed the query letter to the magazine saying I'd like to submit an interview for consideration, along with photos. I got a letter back to send what I had, along with the photos and the magazine would seriously consider my piece. A national magazine! Bravo, me! I now had the ammunition to get the interview. In the meantime, I thoroughly researched everything I could find about him and wrote out thoughtful questions that would make a documentarian proud.

What happened?

I'll tell you.

Romero agreed to an interview, so I bought fresh batteries and new cassette tapes for my tape recorder. Tested my equipment. I had a notebook and fresh ballpoint pens scribble-primed. I even invested in an experienced photographer to capture my Barbara Walters style one-on-one. I cannot remember who provided the photographer recommendation. The blurriness of these facts will make sense in a moment, bear with me.

The photographer was excited. I was excited. We discussed our plan and met in the parking lot of the condominium complex where Showboat Dinner Theatre talent stayed. We rang the doorbell. A few minutes passed and a confused-looking Cesar Romero answered the door in his bathrobe. Clearly embarrassed, he excused himself and closed the door.

The photographer was rattled. He took the incident as an affront to me. He was glad he was there to protect me. He believed the bathrobe was a ruse to solicit sex. I saw a surprised expression by Romero, not a solicitation. But the photographer was clearly concerned for my safety and muttered to me that Romero was an actor and wanted to catch me caught off guard. I appreciated his concern. At the time I didn't believe and still don't believe, anything was a foot. We stopped muttering when we heard the doorknob rattle.

Like any good scene change, Romero opened the door in mere minutes fully dressed and apologized for forgetting, and invited us in. The photographer wasn't so sure. The living room was a typical Florida rental in neutral colors with unmemorable prints in a clean, unlived-in decluttered environment that accommodated minimum stays. I placed my tape recorder on a table positioned between two low back overstuffed chairs that matched the sofa. I introduced the photographer who was teetering between starstruck and suspicious. I decided not to pay attention to the cameraman as I had work to do. He explained he'd move around and take photos. Romero and I should ignore him. We did.

The interview on the following pages is my transcription of the session on February 11, 1982, whereby Romero talked about his career, family, and fond memories with impressive recall for an hour and a half.

Once we left, I asked the photographer to let me know when I could see the photos. He was shooting 35mm film and I expected it would take a few days to develop and get back to me.

He didn't call me immediately, but when he did, he said he was sorry. I was fine, I said, good things take time. No, he said. He forgot to put film in his camera. There were no photos. I didn't think of it then, but I wonder if he didn't put film in his camera or took horribly amateur photos that he would not share. Regardless, we never spoke again. I didn't pay him. He didn't want payment.

I didn't write anything. I felt like a fool. How had I hired someone who couldn't remember to put film in his camera?

I cried. Did nothing. I didn't want to. I never got back to the national magazine. However, I am happy to share the full Q&A here.

Cesar Romero interview February 11, 1982

EW: You said you used to hang around the backstage door at the end of vaudeville shows and watch the performers come out. What did you see in these people?

CR: OH, I was just a stage-struck kid, you know. To me they were very exciting and glamorous people. I always dreamed of being on the stage or being in the movies and stuff like that. I never thought I would be, but I used to love doing anything that had to do with the theater.

EW: How old were you then?

CR: I started that when I was eight. Eight or nine years old when I did a thing in a school play. I went away to boarding school when I was 8 years old school, up in Redding Ridge, Connecticut, Sanford School. One of the older boys in the school was Richard Mansfield Junior, the son of the great Shakespearean actor Richard Mansfield. He was about 18 years old. And that year they gave *The Merchant of Venice* as a school play. His mother, who was also a very well-known actress (Beatrice Cameron) came up to the school and directed the play. Young Mansfield played Shylock. And I did three things in the play. The beginning of the play I was one of the street urchins that ran after Shylock and threw stones at him or something. And another scene, I was the page to the

Moorish Prince who came to woo Porsche. And then the last act I was in the jury in the courtroom scene. And I thought it would be great fun. I'm gonna be an actor. (Laughs)

EW: When did you decide that you wanted to be an (working) actor?

CR: Well, I always had an idea that I wanted to be in show business, but I never thought that it would happen because it was so far from anything in my family. (Taps on the table beside him) My father was the president of an exporting house to Wall Street. And of course, he expected me to go into the business and all that, but unfortunately back in 1922 when I was 14 years old, the sugar market crashed. And my father's business was all the sugar plantations in Cuba. Then the sugar market crashed and ruined my father. He lost everything, so by the time I finished prep school in New York, there was no father's business to go into, and he got me work at the in the National City Bank on Wall Street. One of the vice presidents was a friend of his. I hated it, you know. I did. I didn't like it at all. I've been going around Wall Street with a satchel handcuffed to my wrist, carrying securities. And you know I thought I was gonna get knocked over the head and my hand cut off. (Laughs heartily) But a very good friend of mine, her name was Elizabeth Higgins (Lisbeth), and she was a beautiful dancer. We used to dance well together at all the parties in New York and stuff. She suggested, 'Let's you and I be a dance team.' And we can work at all these wonderful supper clubs they had there in New York in those days. And I thought that would be great fun. So, I used to get together with Lisbeth after I finished working in the bank. We rehearsed some routines and stuff. We went out and gave some more auditions. We got a job in a musical comedy called *Lady Do*.

EW: This was your first break?

CR: Yes. That's what started us off.

EW: Do you feel you were typecast in any particular roles?

CR: I had such a variety of roles in pictures. I've played a lot of gangsters, a lot of foreign characters. I've played a lot of Hindus, Indians, Frenchmen, Latin characters, all types of things. No, I don't think I really was a type. Then of course, I did play the Cisco gig. And the series I did seven or eight of those pictures. But that's what I enjoyed in motion pictures primarily, was the variety. If you have a hit play, you play it year in and year out, night after night doing the same thing. But in pictures, once you've finished the picture there was something else that was completely different. So, you had tremendous variety. It was a great day. It was a great teacher for me, really, because I danced for four years as a ballroom team with Elizabeth and other partners, after that. I got a break as an actor and for the next four years in New York I was working as an actor. But so, my greatest experience in acting actually came from motion pictures because I never had any training of any kind.

EW: You just went right into it?

CR: Yeah. Of course, show business in those days was so different from what it is today. There was much more to show business than there is today. In those days you had not only the theater in New York, but you had burlesque, you had vaudeville, you had nightclubs, you had things that don't exist today. You don't have those great supper clubs in New York anymore, and you don't have all the shows that used to be produced in New York. In those days, every theater in New York had a show. Every type of show, comedy, dramas, musicals, operettas, everything. Today you know you can count them on your two hands. You don't have that training ground.

EW: You said that your favorite film is *Show Them No Mercy*, did you have a least favorite?

CR: (Reflects) Let me see, the least favorite. I don't know. I think, probably some of the pictures that I did at Universal in the early days like *Armored Car* and stuff like that. That were really cheap pictures, *Cheating Cheaters.(Laughs)*

EW: Who were your close friends in Hollywood?

CR: You're probably too young to remember, but George Murphy, Fred MacMurray, Joan Crawford was a very close friend of mine, Agnes Moorehead, Virginia Bruce and Ray Miland.

EW: It was written in the book *Long Live The King* about Clark Gable, that you escorted Carole Lombard to the party where she met Gable.

CR: Not where she met him, but that's the night that the romance really started with them. Yeah, I escorted Carole to the ball, the white ball (charity event). What do they call it? I forget the name of it (charity). She was the chairperson, chair lady, chair, whatever you wanna call it of the ball. She said that all the ladies had to come dressed in white and the men in tails. Of course, everybody did come. Every star in Hollywood was there. In those days it was a very definite motion picture colony then, all came in white except one person. Norma Shearer came in bright red. She said nobody's gonna tell me what to wear. (Laughs) And Carole had a few words to say to Miss Shearer that night. (Laughs) And at one point in the evening, I couldn't find Carole. She'd disappeared.

I said to (inaudible) her great friend and secretary and manager, and I said where the hell's Carole? And she said ohh… She knew. When I finally found Carole, she was with Clark in the corner, in the bar there together talking. You know. And that's what started their romance. They had known each other. They had done a picture before together.

EW: Did you have anybody to which you were really close? That you kind of buddy buddied around with?

CR: Tyrone Power was a very close friend of mine. I had one of the greatest experiences of my life with Ty (Tyrone Power). We both got out of the service after World War II. He was in the Marine Corps. I was in the Coast Guard. I had been on an attack transporter in the Pacific, and Ty was a flyer. We both got out of the service around the same time, and we reported back to the studio and the studio as sort of a welcome back thing or something—also greatly publicized, gave us a little twin-engine Beechcraft. Which Ty flew. And we took off in this little plane and flew down through Mexico and we hit every country in Central America. We circled all of South America. We hit every country in South America except Bolivia and Venezuela. We went down the western coast of Santiago, Chile through and past Buenos Aires and up over Brazil, Guyana, the West Indies to Havana, Cuba. Havana, New York, New York, California, no Havana, Miami. Miami, New York, New York, California. We were ten weeks on this trip. We had our own plan. We had no problems at all. Everything functioned beautifully and we met a lot of interesting people. We met most of the presidents of every country that we went to, because the first person we had to see was the American Ambassador. We had lunch with Peron (President Juan Peron). Evita (first lady and wife of Juan Peron) in Buenos Aires. She was quite a lady. She was a charming woman. When I saw the show (referring to the play Evita). I must say, it brought back a lot of memories. I mean this is something you do once in a lifetime.

EW: What was your family's reaction to Cesar Romero the movie star once you made it?

CR: Ohh, they loved it. My mother loved it all. She was one of the early members of a club that is a very big organization in Los Angeles, Hollywood today called The Motion Picture Mothers Club. It was founded by all the mothers of the people in the motion picture industry, not only actors, but directors and what have you. And they raised a great deal of money every year for The Motion Picture Relief Fund. My mother was one of the first original members of that group, as was Gary Cooper's mother and Tyrone Power's mother and Tom Brown's mother. It was very active with all the mothers of that era. (They) were all members of this and that.

EW: It's still active.

CR: Ohh yes, it's a very big group today and they raise a lot of money for the Motion Picture Country Home and Hospital.

EW: How many other children were there, besides yourself?

CR: I have two sisters and a brother.

EW: Did any go into showbiz?

CR: No, no, my brother is an electrical engineer. My one sister, my older sister was a teacher. She taught Spanish and French and high school for about 8 years. She came out to California off and on. She did a lot of work at UCLA in various departments, in the library, the business office, and the Medical Center and all that. But she hasn't done anything in years. She was always very active in things like that.

EW: Do you feel that growing up in New York City gave you an advantage as to your career choice?

CR: Well in a way it did, because it was the center of show business, New York City. I didn't have to struggle from some little town someplace. You know, come to the big city. I was born there, brought up there.

EW: Of your grandfather Jose Marti, do you like the reference of him being called *the most brilliant of humans*?

CR: He undoubtably was. He was not only one of the great men of Cuba, but of all the Americas. All over Latin America you find statues of him. God, you go to Mexico, any place in South America, Central America, he's one of the great men of this hemisphere.

EW: Do you do you think it's feasible to compare his struggle to see Cuba free from Spain, similar to a young Anwar Sadat's struggle to see Egypt free from Britain?

CR: Any liberator. It's the same thing same as Gandhi was as far as India was concerned. My grandfather struggled all his life. All he did was for the liberation of his country. He was put in chains at the age of 16 for his revolutionary writings in Cuba and put in the in the rock quarry, chopping rocks at the age of 16 with the ball and chain on his leg. The effects of (the chain), which he never got over. We have, my family, the iron rung he had around his leg, connected with the ball and chain. And when my grandmother died of course, then my mother had it. And my mother had all the letters and papers that Marti had written to her and to her sister and brother to my grandmother. A whole stack. All beautifully preserved. They're magnificent letters because he was a prolific writer. And one day my mother said to me 'when I die,' she said, 'I want these things buried with me.' And I said no you can't do that, because I said this is part of the history of a country. You wouldn't bury things that belong to Lincoln or Washington and it's the same thing as far as Cuba is concerned. She said, 'no, no, those things are mine. They're personal.' So, I didn't say anything more. But in 1953 which was the 100th anniversary of Marti's death. (Knocks on the table with his knuckles) President Batista who was still president of Cuba, invited my mother to come to Havana for the Centennial celebrations. And I was gonna go with her but at the last minute I couldn't go because I was assigned to a motion picture, and I had to go to work. So, my sister went with my mother and without saying anything, my mother took all the papers, all the letters and she took the iron rung. And when she was in Havana, she presented them to President Batista. The letters are all in the archives in Havana and the rung is in a crystal urn in the house that Marti was born in the old part of Havana, which is called La Casa de Paula (not sure if this is spelled correctly). It is maintained as a museum. See, he was born in Havana, but his parents were Spanish. His father came from Soria and his mother was from the Canary Islands. His father came to Cuba as a Sergeant in the Spanish Army of Occupation. And their children were born in Cuba. Marti would never allow anyone to call him a Spaniard. He was a Cuban.

EW: Did you ever wish to play your grandfather (on the screen)?

CR: Yes, years ago there was a very fine biography. Because there's so many of them that have been written about him in Spanish and in English, but this one particular book was written by one of the really very fine Cuban writers. He wrote the biography of Marti which my sister wrote a condensed translation of it. She did a beautiful job as a matter of fact. I took it to the studio head of the story department and said this is a story I wish you to consider. I said I'd be very interested in playing, I explained the relationship (Cesar's grandfather being Jose Marti). He sent it back saying, 'well no one in this country knows who he is, and we're not interested in doing biographies.' There was no interest whatsoever. Well, that's true, you see. People in this country (don't know Jose Marti) except maybe yes, around here (Tampa). Yes, because of Ybor City. They go down there and see the terrible little statue of him in that little park. I mean people here, and there's so many Cubans and Latins down there (Ybor). And in most of the country (U.S.), they don't know who you're talking about (Marti). They don't have the slightest idea, because in schools in this country, are never taught anything about Latin American history. At least when I went to school, we were never taught anything about the Latin American countries. So, it wasn't surprising really. (Taps the table)

EW: What do you think of Cuba today?

CR: Ohh, it's a disaster. It's a shame. My God if my grandfather was alive today. He wouldn't… (mutters inaudible). We just had his 129th anniversary. He'd turn over in his grave. In his writings, he said communism is a cancer. Is a cancer on the world. You know Castro quotes him all the time out of context. He claims he (Marti) was the first Cuban communist, which was ridiculous! My grandfather said that communism is a cancer.

EW: Did you ever consider being like him (his grandfather, Jose Marti) in any way? Go into politics?

CR: I wish I could. (Laughs) No way, I haven't got his brains. No. He was a brilliant man. None of it rubbed off on me. (Laughs)

EW: What are your fond memories of your past?

CR: Well, I've had a very good family life. We were a close family, as most Latin families are. Particularly with problems that face them. After this terrible thing happened with my father, where he lost everything and the struggles—they had to keep everything going. They kept me going through private school, which must have been a struggle for them and my sisters, too. You know, to keep things going and all that. My mother, without saying anything to anyone, I found out, was going out and she was playing the piano at a theatrical school, without saying anything to anyone. Of course, it ruined my father. He eventually got Parkinson's disease which some doctors say it can be caused by a tremendous shock to the system. And that very well could have been the cause of my father's illness. Which was a terrible illness in those days, of course. There was nothing they could do for Parkinson's disease. Today there is. Today there's surgery they can do on both sides of the brain and also, they have drugs like L-Dopa (Levodopa), which is very effective with Parkinson's. For my father, there was nothing. He just got worse and worse every year until finally you're just a vegetable. I had a nurse that lived in the house with us, that slept in the same room with my father and took care of him like a child. He was completely incapable of doing anything. He had a rough time, but he was a good man, my father. He did everything he could for my mother. She was a marvelous woman, very talented. She had a magnificent voice, never did anything professionally. She studied music for years. As a young woman she played the piano beautifully, sang all the operas. It was really such a waste. She should have done something, of course, but in her day that was unthinkable. My father had no conception of what it was (performing). He thought people in the theater were not nice people, you know. (Speaks softer) But he lived for a long time to know that it was all ok. He used to love to come to the studio and sit there and watch, you know. He got a lot of pleasure out of it.

EW: Who was your inspiration?

CR: My inspiration. If you can call it inspiration, the fact I had to make something of myself, because I knew I had to do something to take care of my family. And I think that was the thing that kept me going more than anything else. I was determined. I had to do something. I had to because I had to.—I took care of my parents, my sisters, everybody. Put my brother through college, everything. Because I got lucky. (Taps loudly on the table)

EW: Is there anything you would like to change that you've done?

CR: Ohh no. I don't think so because I consider myself very lucky indeed. You know, I've often wondered what would have happened if I hadn't been lucky and things hadn't worked out for me the way they have. I don't know what would have happened. I have no regrets, really, because I consider myself extremely fortunate and particularly now after all the years in the business that I've been. I'm still able to perform and the public still accepts me. This is something that I'm very grateful for.

EW: You've never married.

CR: No, I never married, I had too many responsibilities. I couldn't have somebody come live with my mother, my father, my two sisters, and my two nephews. (Laughs) How about that? You know it takes a long time before the family disintegrated. My father died, and my mother died, my younger sister remarried. By the time I was in my 50s you know, it was too late. I wasn't gonna start getting married then. You get set in your ways and I really don't regret it, at all. I don't regret not having children. I have nieces and nephews. It's the same thing. They cause you just as much trouble. You know there's a saying in Spanish, if God doesn't give you children, the devil gives you nieces and nephews. And they're great. They're all great.

EW: Did you ever have one great love?

CR: Oh yes, everybody's had that. No one that you would know. She was in the business years ago. In her day, she was one of the top singing stars in the country. Unfortunately, people don't remember her, they remember people like Nora Bayes and Ruth Etting. They don't remember Marion Harris. She was one of the top singers of her day. She introduced songs like "More Than You Know," "Time On My Hands." Those were Marion Harris songs. She was the star of *Yours Truly* (Broadway play) with Leon Errol. She was the star of *Great Day* (Musical). She was the star of the show *A Night in Spain*. She died in a hotel fire (Hotel Le Marquis, New York) in 1944. I was overseas. She fell asleep with a cigarette, but that was a long time after she went to London in 1931. And I'd gotten my first break in the theater as an actor. I was playing the lead in the roadshow of the road production of the play *Strictly Dishonorable* in Philadelphia. Marion came to Philadelphia, she said, 'I'm leaving for London I've got a contract over there in Paris and London.' She says, 'so get out of the show and come to London with me.' I said I can't do that. This was the first inkling I've had of any success or anything. I can't do it. She left to London. She just stayed there, lived there for several years and eventually married an Englishman over there and then she came back to this country. She was in a hotel in New York and fell asleep smoking a cigarette.

EW: In the play *The Max Factor* written especially for you, partially by Marcy Rosberg who appeared with you in different plays. I recall seeing photographs of you two together. Do you view your relationship as anywhere close to Kelly Burns and Frederick Howard (the play's characters)? Or your friendship? In other words, are you the lovable idol and inspiration?

CR: She and I are very close friends. There's no romance, there. We're very, very close friends. My God, I you know I'm old enough to her father, or I was gonna say grandfather. (He stops and laughs)

EW: Do you still stay connected?

CR: Ohh, all the time. We see a great deal of each other.

EW: Do you have any hobbies?

CR: I don't have any hobbies. That's why I like to keep working all the time. I think work is my hobby, to keep busy. I can't sit around and do nothing.

EW: You don't have any sports?

CR: I used to play a great deal of tennis and I did a lot of horseback riding, but I don't play tennis anymore. I have a bad back. It goes out very easily, very quickly, and tennis with all the running and all that. Forget it. I don't do very much riding anymore. It's just gotten difficult. Years ago, there were so many places out there that you could ride, you know. Now everything's all built up and the stables and everything are far away. So, you eventually stop doing things. But I don't play golf. I tried it and I hated it.

EW: You still enjoy being a dancer?

CR: No, once around the floor and that's enough. I sit down and watch the others. Well, you know, I used to love to dance because in my day, young people knew how to dance. That was one of the things that everybody wanted to be, a good dancer. Nobody knows how to dance. I'm sorry but they don't. Young people don't know how to dance. They can do all this stuff (gestures his arms), look at each other, you know. What's the fun of pushing somebody around the floor? I'm not gonna get up and wiggle around, do all that stuff. I can't do that. I can, but I won't. I think it's ridiculous.

EW: So, what do you attribute your good health?

CR: I haven't the slightest idea. I try to lead a pretty good life. I keep pretty good hours. I drink in moderation. I don't smoke anymore. I quit that 14 going on 15 years. I think that's probably helped a great deal because I was a heavy smoker. I smoked 3 packs a day. But I don't know. I don't have the slightest. I trust in luck.

EW: Do you consider being around young performers, keeps you in touch with today's Hollywood?

CR: No, not really because I don't know too many young performers anymore. Most of my friends are all gone. Most of them have all died, my really close friends. There are very few of them left.

EW: How do you view Hollywood today?

CR: It's completely different from what it used to be. There is no motion picture industry per se in Hollywood. It's all independent producers. The major studios really don't exist anymore. They're all controlled by conglomerates, big business. Paramount is Gulf

Western. Warner Brothers, MGM, they're all conglomerates. They're not in the hands of the motion picture men like Darryl Zanuck and Samuel Goldwyn and Louis B. Mayer and the Warner brothers and all. That doesn't exist. The big studios are in television production. There is no motion picture colony, the way they used to be. Because within that motion picture colony, years ago, was a very definite society. A very elegant society. The social affairs in Hollywood years ago were fantastic. They're very elegant affairs. Every motion picture star in the industry would be there with, you know, on a list. If you were on that list, you went to everything. And it was a very active social town in those days. That doesn't exist today. Nothing today. The big affairs in Hollywood are all benefits and you don't see anybody there anymore. You don't. None of the big stars today. Who are the big stars, are Dustin Hoffman, Paul Newman, Robert Redford, Eastwood, what's his name (Clint) Eastwood. None of them live in Hollywood. None of them. Paul Newman, they all live in New York, up north. You never see them. Never. You used to see every big star in the business all dressed to the teeth, men in white tie and tails. The women, beautiful. That's all gone.

EW: Do you prefer the (dinner) theater life right now?

CR: It's what I enjoy because this is where I get all the work. If I stayed at home, I'd do a few television things now and then, here and there, and I'd be sitting around most of the time. I can't do that. I have to keep busy. You have to something to do, otherwise you just sit around, get old and die. I know a lot of people that are retired and they're miserable.

EW: You've had a long career. Do you think that it's been a lonely life at any point?

CR: No, my God, no.

EW: Some complain about privacy.

CR: Listen, everybody in this business works to be well known. Don't kid yourselves. They all love it. They might say this and that. But they all love it. You'll put up with whatever you have to put up with. So, people come up and ask you for autographs, and all that. You to go someplace and people see you. I went to the play *4 Girls 4* show at the Bayfront Theatre and from the time I walked in, the whole audience started applauding. You think I objected to that? Thank you. You know I was surrounded with family and friends all my life and I've had no chance to be lonely. On the road sometimes it can be a little lonely, but when you work with people that you like. This show, there are only four of us. We're all close friends. We do things together. It makes it very pleasant. We have dinner together. We do things on Monday, our days off. You're not really alone.

EW: Lastly how do you want to be remembered?

CR: Ohh, Lord. How do I want to be… You know people are here. They're coping with things in life, and they die, and they're forgotten so fast it isn't even funny. Today who thinks of Clark Gable? Today who thinks, yeah, you know I mean, you know I want to be remembered. But I haven't the slightest idea. I think I've led a pretty good life. I try to do the right thing. Uh as far as me and mine are concerned, I have no regrets about anything. I have no regrets that I was saddled with the family because I was. I did what I had to do, and I was happy that I was able to do it. I don't know. I don't think anybody cares. I don't think anybody's gonna give a damn except a few friends I have left. (Laughs heartily)

EW: Did you ever consider writing an autobiography?

CR: No, too many people have done that. I think it's you know. I haven't got the patience to sit down and try to put all things together. Doing that and then, you know I've been approached to do that by couple of publishing (companies). They want a lot of juicy stuff, you know. They want to know all about their sex life. It's nobody's business. No, I have no intentions of writing a book. (Laughs)

EW: Is there anything you'd like to clear up that someone might say later? You never know what they're going to say?

CR: That's a shame, that you know some of these folks like *Mommy Dearest* and things like that come out. I was with Joan (Crawford) when she brought Christina home from the orphanage. Little 6-month-old baby and the love that she put into that child and all the others that she adopted. The three others. I never saw in all the years that I was around Joan, and she was a very close friend of mine. I never saw any act of cruelness to those children. She was strict with them and probably overly strict because she expected perfection from them. And that of course is very deep. You can't really expect that from children, and you couldn't tell Joan. I said they're only kids Joan. They're only children. You can't expect… and she said 'listen, I ain't never had anything when I was a child. I had to work for everything I got.' And she said, 'damn it, these children are going to appreciate what they have.' See, Joan was an abused child. She had to work as a waitress from the time she was eight or nine years old, and all that. She had a terrible childhood. She expected that affection from these children, of course. She had no trouble with the two younger girls, she called twins. They weren't twins at all. They weren't even blood sisters, but they were the same age, and they looked alike. She adopted the two of them at the same time and she called them twins, but they weren't twins at all. She had no problem with them. But she did have problems with Christina and Christopher. And then after Joan died, Christina wrote this terrible book. The last time I saw Christina was in New York, and Joan and I were both in New York and we went and had dinner, the two of us. We had dinner at Christina's apartment. When Christina was married to her first husband who was a director. I can't think of his name now. Their marriage didn't last too long, but Joan and I went up and had dinner with them. We had a charming evening. They couldn't have gotten along more beautifully, you know. I don't know what proceeded that caused Christina to write this book? Whether the fact that Joan left her out of her will or what? She made a lot of money off the book. People that didn't know Joan are going to read this book and say ohh my. That's the way they're going to think of her and forget about this marvelous woman who was such a beautiful person. The terrible book about Errol Flynn that says he was a Nazi spy. They're not here to protect themselves. Another terrible book that was written about Tyrone Power. For God's sake! He was like a brother to me. There was no truth to any of this stuff this guy wrote about Tyrone. He's not here. He's dead. Once you die, anybody can write anything. Nothing anybody can do about it. Not your family. You're dead.

Patrick Wayne

One of John Wayne's cubs is fond of bears

I met Patrick Wayne after one of his St. Peterburg dinner theater performances, September 22nd, 1982. At the time I was a 24-year-old freelance writer, newly engaged and still trying to figure out how to build a writing career. Patrick Wayne, on the other hand, was a working actor with roughly 30 films to his credit and numerous television appearances, who at 43 was a divorced dad trying to keep afloat while raising three kids ages 5, 14, and 16. As I listen to our 1982 interview, I hear the soft voice of a patient man new to performing live.

"I've had a curiosity about the theater for a long, long time," he explained, "but I've had this resistance to do it for a long time." He continues as the servers around us clean up the theater and occasionally rattle dishes. The Country Dinner Playhouse is closed for the evening. It is attached to the Gateway Mall in St. Petersburg, a rival of Dow Sherwood's Showboat Dinner Theater a few miles north. "I'm not quite sure, but I think a lot of it has to do with working in front of an audience. I've never done that before and so I had some questions about it. A sort of this fear of the unknown or something like that." He added, "It's impossible to compare them (movies and television to theater) so I wouldn't

Photo by Emily W. Skinner

even put a preference on one. Motion pictures and television are my primary career. It's where, you know, I make my living." He says *you know* a lot.

Believing my job is to start at the beginning, I gather details. His first acting job was at nine, when visiting his father, the legendary western idol, John Wayne, on set. "The opportunity presented itself and they asked me if I wanted to. And I said what's the deal. They said we'll give you $10 a day and I said okay." He said his parents allowed him to spend his earnings on himself. "That was a lot of money," he laughed.

After college he spent a couple years in the Coast Guard. Then he taught biology for a short stint at Loyola University in Los Angeles, his alma mater. "My strongest inclinations were in the field of biology. If I weren't doing this (acting), that's probably where I would have ended up. When I began college, I took a biology course and was immediately attracted to it. I was an English major and changed and got heavily involved in in the sciences."

When asked if he studied acting, he shared. "I've been in plenty of acting workshops. If you can work all the time, it's great, but that's not the nature of the business, you know. You have to do something the rest of the time to keep the cobwebs out of your head. If you aren't working, you go to classes."

My next question, to be clear, was not flirting. I was sincere. My young reporter self, thought this was a serious question, expecting Wayne might want to break out and try serious roles or more comedy, etc. However, my question came off as cutesy.

"Do feel your natural good looks have caused you to be typecast?" I asked. He sounded a little surprised. Perhaps no one had asked him this before? I thought I was stating the obvious. He took it like a good sport and said, "absolutely."

He rambled on making light of the question and eventually said, "I don't know where I'm going with this." He quickly redirected his focus to the dinner theater performance. "I've been at it less than a year now and it's, you know, it's like a different experience from any kind of acting that I've done before. But it's been, you know, a tremendous experience for me."

Of his film roles (based on his now IMDB.com listings show about 80 total credits), he mentioned two as memorable. "I have several favorites for different reasons. Anyway, one called *Sinbad in the Eye of the Tiger* in which I played Sinbad, was just a wonderful experience for a number of reasons. First of all, we worked in many exotic locations. We were in Jordan and Malta, Spain and London. It's a complete fantasy film. I remember as a child we'd go and see these sorts of swashbuckling films and we'd go home and pick up broom sticks and play like sword fights in the backyard and everything." He added that Sinbad was a childhood fantasy come to life with monsters and beautiful women. Then his voice changes and he fondly shared his experience working on Disney's

The Bears and I. "Ninety percent of the film was just the three bears and myself. We got the bears, just born, you know." (I wished I had asked how they got newborn bears). He said the bears were about six weeks old and had not been trained. "They're just wild. I worked with them for two summers to make it all." He said by the middle filming, "I had developed an incredible rapport with these little animals." Over time he knew how the cubs would respond, and they also seemed to understand how he would. "They became like children, like my children, like people that I know. It was just an incredible experience. There were some wonderful things that happened. I mean it either happens and it works, or it doesn't. So that was, you know, that was gratifying to make."

So many questions now come to mind that I didn't ask, like "what's an example of a wonderful thing that happened? Did you ever visit the bears after the film?" Things I can see myself asking today. As a young interviewer, I couldn't always focus outside of my list of questions and actively listen. With employees trying to close the theater and an actor trying to go home for the evening, I rushed. There wasn't a blueprint for me to follow. I read plenty of celebrity interviews and they all seemed to follow a template of family history, how the interviewee got to this point in their life, and what's next. My journalism teacher taught who, what, where, when, why and how, and to probe for more, but importantly, to get your facts straight.

Like many of the interviews in this book, Wayne talked about the challenges of Hollywood. Others have noted how difficult it is to obtain parts and approval for their performances, but Wayne talked about relationships. He said that living in Hollywood and being in the entertainment industry isn't conducive to maintaining friendships. Friendships in the sense that one calls up their friend to talk or get together when time permits. "The relationships are very strange in this profession. When I say this profession, I'm talking about motion pictures mainly." He goes on to explain that working on location you become a family in for a period with the cast and crew. "You become just intensely involved with people and then you go home. And, you know, your work might take you to some other place. You might not see them (the cast and crew) again for six years and when you see those people again six years later, the relationship is still as intense. It's the quality of the relationships, you know, are as strong and intimate and intense as any relationship you might have." He first relates his experiences to living in Los Angeles, then narrows it to people who work a 9 to 5 job and enjoy weekends with friends. "I can't compare it to living someplace else. So, you know, I don't know what the relationships are, you know, natural normal relationships are like in other places." He adds, "I don't have anything really to base it on. I've never lived anywhere else, you know, I know a lot of people that have spent time in New York and then moved to LA or vice versa or some other part of the world. I was born there, and I was raised there, and that's really the only life I know. I've traveled all over the world. I've spent periods of time in places, you know, met a lot of people in different places."

He continued. He said most of his friends are actors. I used the term stardom when referring to the profession. He surprised me with his candor. "I'm not a superstar. I'm not even a star, in a sense. I mean I have a certain level of visibility, of course. I have my privacy and anonymity, you know. There were times in my life when I could walk down the street and be recognized. That does not happen anymore. I am not recognized anywhere anymore. So, what happens is that you become aware of the fact that people recognize you. And you're on all the time, you know, that you're out there. So, you go into seclusion just, you know, not to be on. I wouldn't call it lonely, but loneliness, aloneness, is self-imposed just for sanity. People create their own lives. It doesn't matter if they're stars."

When asked if he ever considered directing, he said he had more interest in producing. As for his children going into acting, he said he would like them to be happy in whatever they do. Then (I asked, I can't believe I asked this) if women throw themselves at him. He then asks if I'm married, and I share that I'm engaged. He then asks if I'm happily engaged. To which I oddly answer, "it's a new thing for me." Sorry, Tom (my husband who I was newly engaged to when the interview took place and still married to). Patrick Wayne goes on to ask if I've ever been married, and I say no. He asks how old I am and tells me I'm too young to get married. He then shares, "I'm not a person to live alone. I don't really see myself as living the rest of my life alone. I don't see myself living with another person out of marriage either, you know, I come from a different era."

I moved on to talking about his father, John Wayne, the Duke. I led with "I realize that you expect people will ask you about your father." He said, he doesn't expect that. I'm sure my face got red. He went on, "I don't expect it, but, you know, if somebody says they want to interview me, then I think they want to interview me. And sometimes I'm sort of surprised because some people say I'd like to talk to you about your dad, you know, and then I expect it. But if they just say to me, I'd like to interview you, then I really don't expect it. I love my father, you know, I had a lot of great times with him. A really good relationship. I have a great deal of respect for him as an individual as a person but not as a star, as a human being."

Feeling pressured to wrap up, I asked what he wanted to accomplish. "I want to continue to work and grow and be happy doing what I'm doing. I'm not looking to do anything definitive. I want to work. I want to grow. I want to experience, and I don't know where all of that's going to take me. I don't think you can you know. I go out and I do this play here every night, we do it for six weeks or something like that. It's a different experience every night. It's a growing experience. I learn new things about myself. I'm working with the characters that I'm working with. I could do it for 600 weeks and never grow tired of it because it's just, you know, your own life. Whatever's happening to you at that time you can be feeling good. You could feel bad. You could be in love. You could be upset. You could be cranky. I mean anything, you know, to me it's just to be more open. I am open and vulnerable when I'm working, you know."

When the tape was turned off, Patrick Wayne asked me if I would like to sleep with him. I was a bit dumbfounded, but thrilled! OMG! But not because I was interested. Being raised on movie magazines, Mom and I always wondered how celebrities jump from bed to bed, how they ask someone to sleep with them, it was a real curiosity of ours. I wanted to laugh because it was so random. His tone was flat, not seductive. I said, no. He just smiled. It was weird. But I finally got the answer. Celebrities bluntly ask, well, this one at least. Not to be confused with the sexual harassment actors have gone through to get roles. No was no.

I couldn't wait to tell my mother!

Photo of playbill by Emily W. Skinner

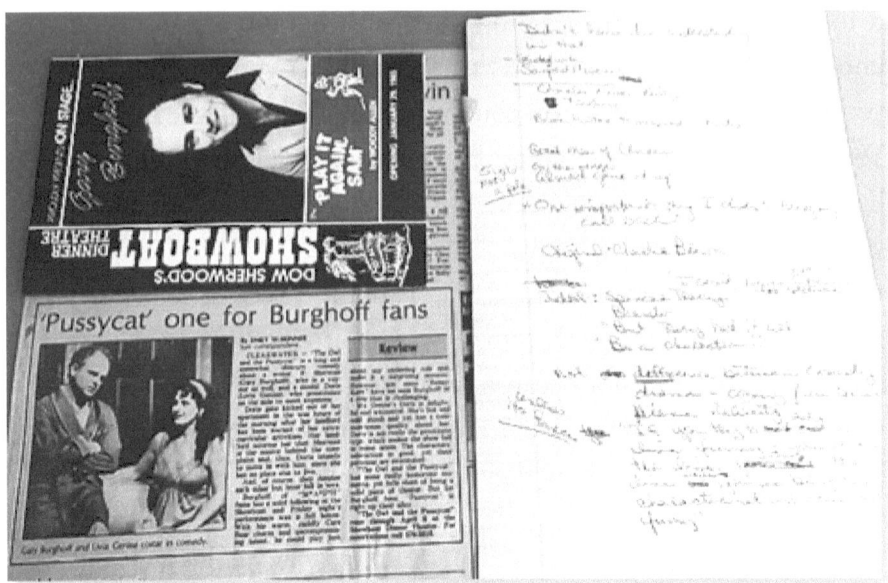

Pictured are a review from The Owl and the Pussycat, a playbill from Play it Again Sam and notes I made during the cassette taped interview with Burghoff. I did my best to have back up materials. Photo by Emily W Skinner

You're a Good Man, Radar O'Reilly

Photo of Emily & Gary taken on Emily's camera by a Showboat Staff member   *Photo by Emily W Skinner*

I met with Gary Burghoff, the actor known for his role as Radar O'Reilly on the Emmy Award winning television series M*A*S*H, Wednesday January 23rd, 1985, 1 p.m. at Showboat Dinner Theatre's office in Clearwater, Florida. Burghoff wasn't scheduled to perform. He opened *Play It Again* a week later on January 29th, 1985. I had hoped to sell the interview to a regional magazine. I didn't. Now, thirty-nine years later a portion of the interview has a home in my memoir. Honestly, I was not a big M*A*S*H fan. I watched it irregularly. War related history interests me somewhat, but mostly movies that showed how we got out of one.

In collecting some background, Burghoff shared that he was born in Bristol, Connecticut and at sixteen his family moved to Delavan, Wisconsin. His soft voice was hard to hear with clarity on my cassette player (all of these years later). He lacks the deeper tones of a Cesar Romero or William Windom, but on the other hand, Patrick Wayne was equally soft-spoken, and we were dealing with dishes being taken up by dinner theatre staff, so I can only conclude that Burghoff was much softer spoken, or my hearing has deteriorated greatly. Actually, both are probably true. Pleasant and low key, he started at the beginning. "I think one of the best organizations in the country is the early Boy's Club," he explained. His mother was actively involved in producing shows for the service organization. "These were big productions that over two weekends the total audience was several thousand people. By the time I was six years old I was beginning to have rapport with an audience." That's when he felt he knew what he wanted to be when he grew up, acknowledging that his post-depression era parents, especially his father, expected him to embrace the importance of a good job. Burghoff attributed his mother's work as the director of the Boy's Club sing party as his inspiration.

"My mother started writing scripts that had spots and lines like original musicals. She was an actress and dancer, an energetic organizer. My dad was a friendly man's man." Not necessarily understanding his son's interest in acting though not completely against it. "A man's identity was having a good job," Burghoff said. "If for some stupid social reason you happen to lose that job, it was part of his identity." Life centered around work. Meaning the stigma of not having a job was greater than why a man found himself unemployed. His parents believed, "You gotta go to college so you can get a good job.—You can't get married. You can't even fall in love until you get a good job. It was a powerful thing that they were instilling," Burghoff said. "I can remember my dad saying to me, after I've been in New York for three years studying acting and not getting a part.—Listen I can get you a job." But Burghoff wasn't ready to give up on his dream. His father chastised, "Oh, you just wanna do what you wanna do." To which Burghoff admitted, "What? I want to do what I don't want to do? Of course I want to do what I want to do."

Studying at HB Studio in NY, and privately with Sanford Meisner and Charles Nelson Reilly, Burghoff attributed his understanding of musical theater to Reilly. "Charles is speaking in classrooms where a musical was like a play. We could actually do a piece of Shakespeare and bring a popular song in and (Reilly) tell the piano player what queue you wanted. Break out in song in a certain place, and you're able to see how you could bring better access to musical comedies."

Burghoff's first big break was the musical *You're a Good Man Charlie Brown*. "I was almost on the verge of giving up. It had been five years studying and auditioning. I didn't get any parts, although I did have some encouragement. I didn't even recognize that being called back was a form of encouragement. When they called me back and said last time I wasn't quite fast enough, or I just wasn't right for it, I felt like I failed." *Charlie Brown* changed all of that. Having played the lead role on both coasts of the United States, Burghoff estimated that perhaps a half million people saw the show.

When asked if he preferred drama to comedy he replied, "I prefer to do both. I have a special fondness for hearing laughter. Comedy is harder. Most of the comedy I do is physical. It has to work. There's no essential difference between drama and comedy,"

Burghoff believed. "Comedy and drama basically come from the same kind of place, reality. If you don't play them for real. If you try to make a funny line. If you try to act funny, you're gonna kill the line," he said. "The author doesn't need help. You just need the character to be real in order for funny lines to be funny."

In working his craft, Burghoff doesn't consider himself a perfectionist, but rather he stated, a detailist, a term he made up. An example of detail he expressed, would be where a strike is going to hit an item in a play, so it can be knocked over at the right time with the right moment. Once that is established, acting technique can start without fear. "I take care of the comedy first, you know, detail upon detail then we work on acting technique."

Of the actors Burghoff most admires he said Marlon Brando and Spencer Tracy. "I could never hope to attain his (Tracy's) stature. Tracy was not one of these handsome guys. He was a character actor. There are subtle differences with each of his roles. Differences that made them stronger. I mean he was not a personality. He was a dynamic person. The characters he played were researched from his own experience. He (Tracy) never liked to talk about acting. He said just learn your lines. What he was really saying, you know, is just be it (the character). Be the character. Not everybody knows how to do that, some of us have to talk about it in order to understand it."

After M*A*S*H the film and the television series, he did a pilot for the Radar character. "I really didn't want it," Burghoff said. "The studio kept after me to do it. They offered me $75,000 for one week's work and I had nothing to lose. I kept telling them I don't think that it's right for me to do this. I went in there and I did the very best that I had always done. Then I think they probably realized that I was a little older, that I may have been beyond it. A local paper said that I was one of those people who made a big mistake by leaving a successful television show." A decision Burghoff doesn't regret. He wanted to spend more time with his family. And while he was open to films, he said it's very hard when casting identified him with a single character, Radar.

As for other interests, Burghoff shared, "All the aptitude tests that I took from the State of Wisconsin said that I should write. I have not the discipline to go through the same kind of training and dedication that I did for acting—five intense years in New York. I don't think at this point in my life that I wanna do that. I'm lazy. I've got a very good thing going with the acting."

Reflecting on his earliest memory of being a six-year-old on stage, "When I heard people laugh at something, some vulnerability that I'd exposed on stage, I realized they're (the audience) laughing because they have the same vulnerability. They may never have shown me that vulnerability on the street or at the office or whatever, but it's there. That's a very good feeling."

In total, I saw Burghoff in three plays. I reviewed his Showboat performance in *The Owl and the Pussycat*. I preferred him in *Play It Again Sam* and an earlier production, *Boney Kern,* not that my opinion matters. And while he was a super nice guy to interview, I struggled to put this chapter together. I almost didn't include it.

Comedian Jay Leno prescribes dose of fresh humor

SATURDAY, October 26, 1985
Clearwater Sun, SunLiving, Section B
By EMILY SKINNER
Sun correspondent

Jay Leno, one of comedy's hottest properties these days, is not your typical "take the money and run" celebrity.

The 35-year-old comedian, who will appear regularly on NBC's "TV's Bloopers and Practical Jokes," doing what he calls a man-on-the-street segment, has an easy manner that makes you feel as though he were the next-door neighbor or the local mechanic. He seems to enjoy talking about himself and doesn't feel the need to be "on" all the time.

A one-time mechanic himself, Leno began his comic career in Boston, his hometown, working for an auto dealership in the daytime and doing stand-up in the evenings.

And, unlike many of his counterparts, Leno would rather make his living traveling the comedy club circuit and doing occasional spots on "Late Night With David Letterman," as well as his spot on "Bloopers," than do a string of specials or record albums.

In fact, Leno hasn't and doesn't intend to do any albums.

"I think its's more of an ego thing when someone does an album," Leno said. "If someone wants to hear my act they can come and see me."

Unlike Bill Cosby and other comedians who have "classics" albums that are collector's items. Leno still doesn't feel the necessity to record some of his favorite or choice material.

"I'm just not comfortable with it (recording)," he explained. "Now I can see someone like when Steve Martin decided that he wasn't going to go on the road anymore, he made an album. Now I can see that.

"But I can't really see putting all your material on an album… I mean there has to be some mystery to it—otherwise, it's overexposed to death.

"In the old days, Jack Benny and other comedians honed their act for four or five years. That's the craft. It's like you can't record (do) topical material—Reagan was in Jersey—it really gets dated."

As for cable specials. Leno does have one in the works. He currently is working on a Showtime special, "Jay Leno and the American Dream," which should air in January.

"I don't think it's fair for the audience to see me on TV doing my routine and come see me that night when I am in town and hear the same thing," Leno said.

"If I'm on the Letterman show and do some jokes, I won't do them for eight months (while touring). I like to know where my act is," the comedian explained.

Having appeared on "Late Night" about 27 times. Leno and a handful of other comedians are frequent guests of the zany nocturnal program.

"TV is like craps," Leno said. "If you're on Letterman and you are funny, they ask you back in a couple months. So you go back and if you are funny again, they ask you to come back."

Keeping, with his tight schedule of the comedy club appearances, Leno feels that working every day is the easiest way to break in new material. He doesn't feel it necessary to write out or rehearse his material previous to performances.

"It's like when I was in college. I don't study a lot, but I show up for class," the comedian said.

Leno also avoids doing sexist jokes. "I've never liked sexist jokes. If you have four or five women sitting at a table and you do Dolly Parton or women driver jokes… there is a coolness," Leno said.

"It's like I was doing a show and I asked this one woman what she did. And she said she was an attorney. Well, I did some attorney jokes and then after the show she said to me, "I'm really glad you didn't make any jokes about my being a woman attorney."

It appears Jay Leno will continue honing his craft, taking care that his audiences receive a fresh dose of Leno humor at each stop. And how does he feel about the future?

"I feel each comedian has five great years. And for me, each year gets better. I feel my five years are coming up."

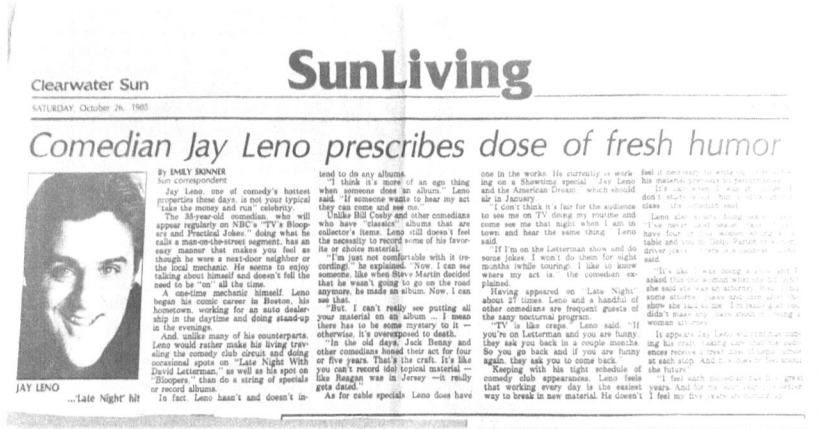

Portfolio Article Photo by Emily W Skinner

Bohemian Chronicle
1991-1995

Photo by Emily W Skinner

I originally wrote a few paragraphs about this period deeming it my self-indulgent hobby. Then I unearthed the Bohemian Chronicle archives to have a look and discovered we'd actually done something. For those who want to see every issue, look at the Bohemian Chronicle Facebook page.

With the evolution of AOL *American Online*® dial-up internet connections, chat rooms, *MTV*®, *Ebay*®, the flip phone, and the reemergence of coffee shop culture like *Starbucks*® from about the late-1980s to mid-1990s, also arose the comeback of the zine. Not a magazine, but something akin to pamphleteer publications. The zine dates back as far back as the 1930s. Mental Floss reports that in 1993 there were about 40,000 zines published in North America. https://www.mentalfloss.com/article/88911/brief-history-zines "Most definitions of zines include the fact that they are small-circulation, self-published, and often inexpensive or free." The article goes on to say, "The most important aspect of a zine is generally that the publication identifies as one. Many zine-makers will say zines are as much about the community as the product, and that identifying as a zine is what separates these publications from comics, literary journals, websites, and other types of independent publications." Our *Bohemian Chronicle* was one.

After Tom and I made two attempts at entrepreneurship (don't ask), not to mention my freelance writing career (which is all you have been reading about), it became obvious that our two children deserved a more secure existence. We'd already purchased term life insurance, were paying our mortgage on time, and taking the kids regularly to the beach, library, and our Catholic church's crying room, when we determined one of us had to get the "good job" with benefits. Mind you, my husband became a Mr. Mom before it was the norm, so you know who scored the benefits package.

As our family's breadwinner, I no longer wrote but worked nights in the Valpak coupon factory in Largo, Florida as a proofreader, later as a nightshift supervisor of a team of graphic artists, composers and proofreaders, and then as a sale representative. Almost immediately I felt creatively withdrawn. Well, not dramatically withdrawn in a scary way, but slightly depressed. I needed something to do when I got home at 1 a.m. or 3 a.m. as I couldn't wake my sleeping people to play a board game or watch a movie. I needed a hobby to unwind. I missed writing.

So, I decided to create a zine to fill the wee hours. We (myself, my sister Ellen, and her high school best friend/roommate at my mother's house, Linda, who would later marry our brother Mark and produce our niece Sara and nephew Nathan) wrote the launch issue. Soon after, we received submissions from friends and coworkers hungry to get published—as well as creatives outside of our peer and work relations. So, we opened a post office box (no longer open) to receive queries and after work, I'd review submissions, write rejection or acceptance letters and go to bed. Ellen and Linda would come over once a month to read, edit, type, write or paste-up while I was still asleep and Tom and the kids were at the park playing.

As a team we decided what stories we liked and tried to have some kind of theme each issue. Once all was typeset, I'd get the zine copied at *Staples* on a unique paper color for that month, then saddle-staple them. Next, we'd all deliver new editions to coffeehouses, laundry mats, and free racks. Later we'd develop relationships with folks who would distribute our publication to their community, on a naval ship, a parsonage, libraries, coffeehouses, etc. And in due course we sold some subscriptions in an attempt to cover a portion of the mailing costs.

When our listing hit the *Writer's Market* publications and *Long Ridge Writers Group*, more and more submissions arrived from writers and artists as far as Israel, Saudi Arabia, England, Japan, New Zealand, Australia, as well as U.S. cities and at least one prison. It became an unpaid job that soon stretched the boundaries of a pastime. The *Bohemian Chronicle* was no longer *my* outlet, but a channel for frustrated artists and writers who wanted to be in print, and as such, I became a frustrated publisher who took herself way too seriously at times. But not quite as serious as a demanding artist who showed up at our house and expected, then begged to be in the next issue. My husband sat with me at the kitchen table during negotiations, mostly to get the guy to leave, but also to back me up. But this guy wasn't the only bruised ego to protest our rejection. We had a policy of providing feedback and our feedback wasn't received well by professors and well-established authors who enlightened us to the fact that they were the head of an English department or had once received praise from Kurt Vonnegut and any laundry list of acceptances, often enclosing a record of every publication in follow-up correspondence. It was baffling to hear these objections, as we had none of their credentials. Please, move on!

A letter of apology. *The notable dean wordsmith misunderstood your comments as his recent eye surgery had rendered our handwritten comments undistinguishable. Or the tenured fellow was experiencing exhaustion from a taxing test period and misread…* Okay, I've exaggerated.

But we also received a lot of thank you notes and praise, even a nomination for *Writer's Digest's* "Fiction 50" in 1994. All *Chronicle* issues were typed on my Commodore 64, later upgraded to an Amiga computer that our four-year-old wiped clean in a matter of minutes as soon as it was set up and all floppy disc archives transferred. Blair played at typing—so cute. Live and learn. Nine-year-old Marquel was not as interested in the computer. She wrote poetry and drew pictures we'd include in a few issues. Since our dot matrix printer had font limitations, we relied on old-school transfer letters we'd scratch onto our paste-up templates. This meant buying multiple packs of transfer letters to have backup, since we never knew what our headline needs would be. We got complaints about inconsistent fonts and font sizes from a handful of readers. Our zine was a channel long before blogs were a thing, a time capsule of the 1990s with stories, art, poetry that reminds us today of the AIDS epidemic, the Bosnian war, Hurricane Andrew and more.

I became a jerk at times. I'd wake up at noon after coupon production overtime, and instead of being thankful there were several women reading, drinking coffee, chatting and typing in our Florida room, I'd stumble out in my robe to ask them to break up the merriment and get to work. Mind you, I was sleeping in a hot room with a ceiling fan and they were enjoying a wall unit air conditioner, so I think I may have been sleep deprived. I ran them off, of course. My sister tolerated my rants, my sister-in-law not so much. But that didn't keep us from working together. Eventually the three of us would write a screenplay over a long weekend holed up in a transient motel not far from my house—and created some public access television shows that were a mix of sketch comedy like *SNL* and *Kids in the Hall* mixed with *American Bandstand* dance segments. Pretty much along the lines of *A Black Lady Sketch Show* well before its time, but we were white ladies and my husband as our male filler character. Tom had a fairly decent part-time acting career for a non-Orlando based actor. Orlando had Disney-MGM and Universal Studios that came into vogue in the 1990s while the rest of Florida was striving to keep pace. Tom's best gig was stand-in work for then *Cop Rock* star Peter Onorati—on a CBS Movie *With Hostile Intent* (an original network movie before streaming when cable television was still in its

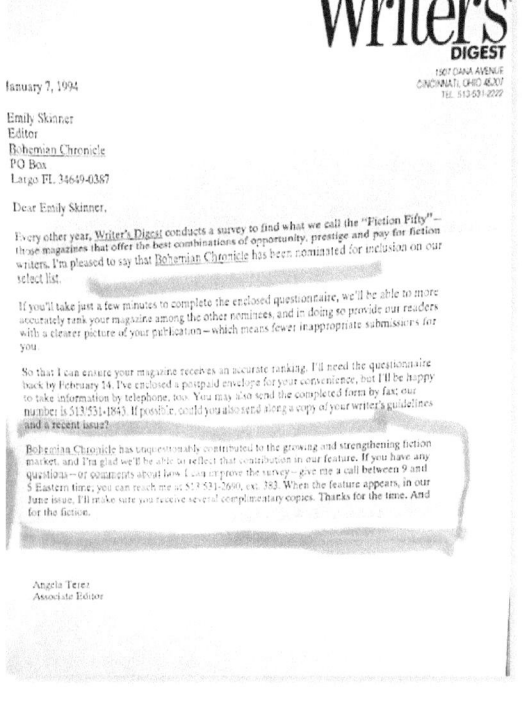

infancy). It was shot in Tampa. Tom also got some local commercials which paid modestly and added some credits to his resume.

We were women making things happen long before smart phones and social media made it easy. Thanks to our friend Dorie Cox's helpful suggestion, we took television production classes at our local Vision Cable studio and checked out equipment to create content only a few watched. One being a Valpak manager, John Pask, who said he was tired of seeing me on his television at 3 a.m. after we'd all finished overtime.

We won Best Avant-Garde Programming for *Dance* at the 7th Annual Community Access Spotlight Achievement Award, June 30th, 1993. Many of those who attended the six prior awards informed me that we pissed off a guy who took the avant-garde prize several years in a row because he had no competitors.

But nothing can or will compare to what my daughters, real women in film, do. Blair has worked for *Oscar, Emmy* and *Golden Globe* award-winning films and shows in a variety of jobs including producer and production supervisor. She and Marquel (our actress/director/producer) with credits on network television and streaming content have created also their own unique films and web series, *Ana Mead, Pleasant Pastures, Eleanora: The Forgotten Princess,* and *Stand-Up Girls* to name a few. And as such, they made the booktrailer for my novel *Marquel*. Additionally, we collaborated on (they produced, directed, and starred in) the only short film I've written (to be made), *Dough Nuts, and More*.

My stint at publishing would eventually lead to self-publishing my own books, as I don't have patience to send out queries. Anything outside of a real job, I've adapted my own strategy. Suffice it to say, I've proven perhaps the best way *not* to do things.

Accepting the Vision Cable Award – Photo provided by Vision Cable PR *Photo by Emily W Skinner*

My sister Ellen Williams & friends Dorie Cox, Jessa Goodwin & Michele Belisle in South Florida to help the victims of Hurricane Andrew, August 1992.

Bohemian Chronicle Cover Photos & Article Photos on this page by Emily W Skinner

An article about an artist, Sithembile, in Zimbabwe. Her cover art below. I bought the watercolor pictured in the story. It hangs in my livingroom.

IF YOU'RE CHICKEN, HE WILL COME

by Ellen M. Williams

Everyone admires someone, and when "Building the Perfect Beast" came out I found an ally in this cold world. He understood how it felt to be hurt by love, life and society's ever constricting limitations. Don Henley would always know what to say.

The connection sustained me until 1989's release, "The End of the Innocence". I knew I had to talk to him. I just couldn't afford to hop a plane to LA or Aspen and hang out in his favorite eateries until I found him. Luckily, he came to me. (He didn't know he was coming to me, but I did.)

6/27/90, Wednesday, around 5PM-EST: In two days Henley would be performing to a crowd of 30,000 within screaming distance of my back yard and I was getting restless. Would I be meeting him or not? His management couldn't say...

Meanwhile, it's 110 degrees in LA; Henley's pissed because the a/c at his house is broken. While I'm hanging on the phone, he's waiting downstairs (at H.K. Management) in a limo to go to the airport.

"Oh, is he coming to Tampa International tonight?"

"No, Orlando," was the simple reply.

"Oh." Thanks bye gotta go.

So it was on the assumption that a commercial flight would bring destiny near that I kidnapped my quite willing sister-in-law to accompany me on a vision quest. In an effort to remain calm, we verbally assaulted ourselves during the 100 mile drive for being so spontaneous; we knew nothing would come of it but wasted time watching planes like idiots. But that wouldn't stop us from trying.

Once there, we scouted a monitor listing arrivals. There were no flights from LA, in fact, there was only one flight arriving from anywhere that night. It came from Atlanta.

Don Henley, along with his band, his crew, and a few other people who actually had some other reason for travelling that night, approached us from Gate 47. We immediately became paralyzed from the neck up.

This was really happening, and we were there.

We wandered aimlessly past the crowd. I stared outright at Don, making a commitment to myself that our eyes would meet. I'm not sure about my expression, but when I think back I picture Rasputin in a denim skirt and hi-tops.

We turned, following our quarry at a discreet distance. My honest impression of the man was that he was a normal person; a handsome, slightly disheveled human being who just so happened to be a musical genius and a superstar. I was relieved and awed.

My sister-in-law and I spoke in hushed expletives. We were wallowing in mutual uncertainty, fear of embarassment and the lack of anything intelligent to say. In desperation our steps grew larger, and we got as close to Don as we dared. (Close enough to discover that his jeans were indeed Levi's and his butt's a little flat.)

He was the last of his kind to get on the escalator to the baggage claim. We hadn't the strength to join him, so we bypassed the escalator. As he glanced over his right shoulder, his eyes met mine for the last time. Unfortunately, he looked paranoid. Kind of a "They ARE following me!" thing.

I never got to talk to Don. Somehow I thought a night in the Orlando airport wouldn't be my only opportunity.

Henley continued on next page

Photo of Bohemian Chronicle paste up by Emily W Skinner

Is Rape Fashionable?

By Emily W. Skinner
Bohemian Chronicle
October 1992

What are the fashions of rape?
Do women dressed in sexy attire really ask to be raped?
*1 On Nov. 6, 1988, a 22-yr.-old woman wearing a white lace mini-skirt, a green tank top and no underwear alleged that she was kidnapped from a Fort Lauderdale restaurant parking lot at knifepoint and raped twice.

The jury who heard this case decided the defendant was not guilty on the grounds that the woman had solicited sex.

"We all feel she asked for it for the way she was dressed," explained jury foreman Roy Diamond.

This prompted Florida lawmakers to add a provision to the existing Sexual Battery Statute which reads

794.022 Rules of evidence

(3) Notwithstanding any other provision of law, reputation evidence relating to a victim's prior sexual conduct or evidence presented for the purpose of showing that manner of dress of the victim at the time of offense incited the sexual battery shall not be admitted into evidence in a prosecution under s.794.011 or s.794.041.

So what happened in the most celebrated case brought forth by the media and televised to an audience worldwide?

In the William Kennedy Smith trial, we saw Patricia Bowman's bra passed around the jury, her pantyhose and dress examined by several expert witnesses who studied the clothing for grass samples and fabric damage and we also heard Kennedy's attorney Roy Black imply that she had incited the rape by removing her pantyhose.

*2 "You were interested enough to go in the house with him?" Black asked.

"I was more interested in the house than him," she (Bowman) said.

"Interested enough that you took off your pantyhose?" Black asked.

Why didn't the rules of evidence apply in this case?

In a recent phone interview, Assistant State Attorney Moira Lasch explained that she had filed a motion under s.794.022 and that the motion was denied by Judge Mary Lupo. She added that Roy Black had said that the clothing would prove to be the most important piece of evidence in the case. Lasch suggested we call Judge Lupo's office and find out why the motion was denied.

Ruthann Kravetz, a Judicial Assistant in Judge Lupo's office returned our call. Both she and Lasch asked not to be quoted directly because each was drawing from recollection and not the case file.

Kravetz explained that the motion was denied and the clothing allowed into evidence under the grounds that it would prove that a struggle the victim alleged had occurred would have meant the clothing sustained significant damage and not that the clothing had incited the rape.

So why or how did Roy Black get away with suggesting that the victim had incited the rape by removing her pantyhose?

Is Rape Fashionable?

The court records are available in Palm Beach County and though we did not travel the distance to view the thick files, we relied on the print media's (newspapers and magazines) version of what happened. As it turns out we cannot find an objection by Moira Lasch or any instructions by Judge Lupo to ignore Black's remarks. It doesn't mean that these did not take place, but rather the media had no comment or concern for Statue 794.022 and the motion filed by Lasch.

How can we as citizens express our concern and disgust at this obvious obstruction of justice? As Lasch put it, if there is no conviction, there is no grounds for appeal.

Clothing is evidence in sexual battery cases. It is used primarily for the purpose of gathering semen, sperm, hair or blood samples. But how this evidence is used in a court of law really isn't defined. Patricia Bowman's bra was never mentioned in Smith's testimony as Lasch pointed out, yet it was passed around for the jurors to touch and examine.—And what importance was it to note that Bowman's dress was purchased at Anne Taylor or that her undergarments were purchased at Victoria's Secret, unless it is to establish that Victoria's Secret sells suggestive clothing or rape attire?

*3 "The FBI sought to establish how many rape victims had 'asked for it.' To do so, they defined 'victim-provoked rape' as any rape before which the victim has smiled at the rapist, talked to him, accepted a drink or a ride, dressed provocatively or done anything at all which could conceivably have led the rapist to believe she was willing."

Their finding was that only 4% of rapes were victim-provoked?

What other crimes are considered victim-provoked? Is murder or child abuse a victim-provoked crime?

*2 "You were interested enough to go in the house with him?" Black asked.

"I was more interested in the house than him," she (Bowman) said.

While our legislators are trying to make the term *victim-provoked rape* a definition of the past, it is unfortunate that its theory and relevance is very much alive in our nation's courtrooms.

1. Jet May 14, 1990
2. St. Petersburg Times, Dec. 6, 1991
3. Avoiding Rape -Without Putting Yourself In Protective Custody, The Athena Press 1982

Marquel Booktrailer—Eric Roberts

I debated whether to put this in the Harry Whittington section of the book, because he approved the outline and sample chapter of my novel *Marquel,* which ultimately led to my publishing the book. However, the booktrailer has nothing to do with Harry, though I think he would have loved the advent of short form film trailers to publicize a novel. My daughters read the book when they were college age and of course didn't think much of it. Marquel randomly mentioned to her talent manager, Robert Enriquez, that her mother had authored a novel using her name. Intrigued, he read the book and liked it. He thought a booktrailer might serve as a trailer to pitch a movie. Eric Roberts was cast as Dr. Zach Manning, opposite my daughter, Marquel. Blair directed.

Made in 2012 in California while I was home in Florida selling coupon advertising, everyone consulted me and kept me in the loop. We released it on Youtube with social media posts. Today it has a little over 3,000 views. Not a viral sensation, but author Lee Goldberg said (12 years ago) that it was the best booktrailer he'd ever seen. That was a bright spot. I finally had the chance to meet Eric Roberts at Pensacon comic con in Pensacola, Florida, February 2023 when he was doing a meet-and-greet signing photos. At Pensacon, my husband took the photo you see on a subsequent page. Roberts was super nice and has a great sense of humor. Once I showed him the updated novel and asked him to sign the page that included his photo from the booktrailer, he graciously did and added "I love you and your family." He may sign others' photos that way. I don't know. Regardless, he made my day! My daughters and their partners also gifted me a 2020 Mother's Day *Cameo* video from Carson Kressley of *Queer Eye for the Straight Guy* fame. Kressley speaks to the novel's character Ken Avery, a Hollywood agent. I told my daughters if a movie was made, I wanted Kressley to be Avery. After Covid lockdowns they learned about https://www.cameo.com and made my dream come true in the sense that Kressley talked about wanting to be Ken Avery. Thank you! To see the Cameo https://www.youtube.com/watch?v=1oGNwr-RhjY

Photos by R. J. DeGuzman

My daughters during the production of the booktrailer for my novel, *Marquel*.

You can watch the booktrailer on YouTube www.youtube.com/watch?v=6e6O7iYqeVQ

Marquel Skinner as Marquel. Eric Roberts as Dr. Zach Manning.

Book page and author mobile by Emily W. Skinner

Photo of Eric Roberts & Emily Skinner by Tom Skinner.

To see the Carson Kressley Cameo https://www.youtube.com/watch?v=1oGNwr-RhjY

Screenshot Photo of Carson Kressley by Emily W Skinner

Photo of Eric Roberts' signature on a copy of my updated novel Marquel at Pensacon, February 2023, Pensacola, FL by Emily W. Skinner.

Masterclass.com = Aaron Sorkin

Before I start, let me say that I am not receiving any remuneration from Masterclass.com nor James Patterson, David Mamet, David Baldacci, Dan Brown, Margaret Atwood, Shonda Rhimes, Ken Burns, nor Aaron Sorkin for my endorsement of their individual classes and the Masterclass.com brand. I was an original enrollee of Masterclass.com and enjoyed wonderful communication with a guy named Brad who interacted with subscribers. As such, I answered lots of questions and provided my preference of experts, Aaron Sorkin was at the top of the list. As a writer and budding screenwriter, I bought Sorkin's class as soon as it was added. In the early days, Masterclass.com offered individual classes vs. the subscription model.

I started with James Patterson's class. He reminded me of working with Harry Whittington. Also, Patterson's editing exercises are helpful for experienced and new writers. As a fan of David Mamet's plays and films, most especially *Glengarry Glen Ross* and *House of Games,* I appreciated his serious no nonsense approach to story. Baldacci's class enlightened me on how our conspiracy theories are not that far-fetched from F.B.I. and government tested programs.—Because I love symbolism, Dan Brown was a writer I hoped would teach-to-the-topic, but instead he surprised me with details on his outlining and story development. Brown is a great tactician and a must-take class for new writers. He was very generous with his practices, while Margaret Atwood and Shonda Rhimes proved to be more protective of their method. Ken Burns taught me that a floor sweeper interested in on-the-job documentary training can become a reliable team member and as such, be counted on for future projects. Burns also explained his process of visual storytelling through the use of photos when interviews and video aren't available.

On to Aaron Sorkin, what I loved about his video introduction is the difficulty he had articulating on camera. The Master of Television and Movie Dialogue, the writer of *A Few Good Men*'s "You can't handle the truth" monologue told his class that if he could type out his introduction it would be better. What a relief! I have the same affliction. The words don't flow in my brain-to-mouth connection the way my brain-to-hand connection performs. I took Public Speaking in junior college and even competed in persuasive, informative, and entertainment categories with my best results in persuasive speaking. I discovered that I'm better off being fired up about something. So, thank you Aaron Sorkin for making me aware that I am not alone.

And speaking of Brad, the Masterclass.com facilitator extraordinaire, I raised my hand when an opportunity came to ask Aaron Sorkin a question. It's still there in the lesson if you take his class. I saved a sound recording to listen to when I want to pinch myself for this moment.

My Q.
Aaron Sorkin's A.

E: When you get feedback (on a screenplay) from someone with experience and expertise, coverage, but you disagree with the notes, what do you do?

A: You be polite. What you've just described has happened to me any number of times and it will happen to you any number of times. You're going to be in a situation where, you know, Steven Spielberg says, gee I think it should be blue. But you really believe it should be red.—What I would do is press on them a little bit. Be honest, say, you know, I disagree. Here's why. Tell me why I'm wrong? You know, make them make their case and if they don't make their case, if you still believe in what you're doing, then do what you're doing. Because I'm sure that's how Steven Spielberg got to be Steven Spielberg. I'm using this ridiculous example of Spielberg, but now that I think of it, it's not that ridiculous. Absolutely no one wanted Steven Spielberg to make Shindler's List, *okay. I was there. Absolutely no one wanted him to make it. He was allowed to make it in exchange for making* Jurassic Park, *okay. So, he was right and everybody else was wrong.*

E: Thank you!

A: You bet.

L-R Julie Nunis, Kevin Gardner, Blair Skinner, Jim Fath, Marquel Skinner, Desi Stein, & Shirley Jordan
Cast photo by R.J. DeGuzman

Dough Nuts And More is a dark comedy about Jane Dough, a superstar sales rep/super mom whose big sales presentation is disrupted by a call that her accident prone husband is in the hospital, again.

This is Emily Skinner's first short film script. Her daughter Marquel Skinner plays Jane Dough and directs. Her daughter Blair Skinner produces and makes a cameo appearance.

Dough Nuts And More

My one and only script-to-screen achievement, thanks to my daughters Marquel and Blair, is *Dough Nuts And More*. Many thanks also to the cast and crew of the short film. We were nominated Best Comedy Short at Sunscreen Film Festival 2019.

I wrote this after my diabetic schoolteacher husband didn't answer his cellphone on a busy sales day. I was between appointments at my day job selling coupon advertising and just wanted to vent to someone. Tom didn't answer his phone as he often plays games, watches Youtube videos, Tweets or whatever, and misses my text messages, calls, his phone's voicemail alerts, or has his ringer off. You'd think he is trying to ignore me, right?

So, on this particular day I imagined the worst. I wasn't worried, I was angry! If you want to see how my mind works, watch *Dough Nuts And More* on Vimeo https://vimeo.com/280220994.

Author Haunts
Homes, Graves, Museums

One of my favorite pastimes is to visit author landmarks. I also collect author biographies, autobiographies and self-published regional history that provide resident lore and narratives that's often not Googleable. When I watched Bishop Barren's video about Flannery O'Connor as part of his *Word on Fire* Catholic series, I noted the author's home, Andalusia, in Milledgeville, Georgia. Milledgeville is also home to the ruins of the infamous historic mental hospital, Georgia State Lunatic Asylum founded in 1842 later renamed Central State Hospital. As I toured Andalusia, I picked up a biography about O'Connor that gave me a better perspective of her town. Connor is on my list of Southern Literary Women, along with Margaret Mitchell, Zora Neale Hurston, Harper Lee, and Margorie Kinnan Rawlings. What follows are some of my favorite stops.

Algonquin Hotel, New York City, NY 1983

I was unaware of the Algonquin, until my creative writing teacher said my writing (class assignment) reminded her of Dorothy Parker who was a member of the Algonquin Round Table.

If you are unfamiliar here's Brittanica.com definition.

"Algonquin Round Table, informal group of American literary men and women who met daily for lunch on weekdays at a large round table in the Algonquin Hotel in New York City during the 1920s and '30s. The Algonquin Round Table began meeting in 1919, and within a few years its participants included many of the best-known writers, journalists, and artists in New York City. Among them were Dorothy Parker, Alexander Woollcott, Heywood Broun, Robert Benchley, Robert Sherwood, George S. Kaufman, Franklin P. Adams, Marc Connelly, Harold Ross, Harpo Marx, and Russell Crouse. The Round Table became celebrated in the 1920s for its members' lively, witty conversation and urbane sophistication. Its members gradually went their separate ways, however, and the last meeting of the Round Table took place in 1943."

I was a college student when my teacher made the Dorothy Parker comparison. A generous compliment. Thank you, Martha Roland of St. Petersburg Junior College for the encouragement! Roland included my humor short *Under the Mat* in the college's literary magazine, *Obelisk,* as well as providing me one of SPJC's fellowships to USF's three-day Florida Suncoast Writers Conference.

When my then fiancé (now husband of 40 plus years) asked where we should honeymoon, I chimed, "Algonquin Hotel in New York!" I secretly hoped Dorothy's ghost might linger in the hotel's lounge as we honeymooned. To give you an idea of her sharp wit: *A hangover is the wrath of grapes. If love is blind, why is lingerie so popular? If you don't have something nice to say, come sit by me.* Dorothy's ghost didn't materialize downstairs, but a fire alarm did go off on our floor followed by a frantic scene of people roaming the hallways in their bathrobes. Then the alarm stopped abruptly and everyone returned to their rooms. Hmm.

Tom & Emily Skinner. Photo by Blair Skinner

On our 30th anniversary we returned and dined at the hotel's restaurant. Photo above.

Monroeville, Alabama—Harper Lee & Truman Capote
May 9, 2014

When I discovered Monroeville, Alabama's annual performance of Harper Lee's *To Kill A Mockingbird*, I had to go! The play takes place inside and outside of the courthouse where Lee's father tried cases, now the Monroe County Heritage Museum. The museum includes Truman Capote displays, too. The two literary legends were childhood friends and Capote, the basis for Dill in *Mockingbird*, grew up in Monroeville and as such, when their community needed to raise funds to restore the old courthouse in 1991, museum director, Kay McCoy came up with the idea of a one act play of *Mockingbird*, their website reports. The show was successful enough to travel abroad and grow into a full-length play. The museum is both a shrine to the Harper Lee and Truman Capote, and a set for the play when in season. To learn more about their annual schedule go to https://www.tokillamockingbird.com/.

The town's people, not professional actors, perform each year for several weeks and do an amazing job. Having seen Aaron Sorkin's adaptation on Broadway, I'd say the Monroeville residents are on par with the professionals. Sorkin reworked the child parts as adult Scout, Jem, and Dill. We enjoyed both, but if I had to choose one, I'd choose the Monroeville performance. It's very emoting to see a local resident in the role of Tom Robinson, the accused. It's equally disturbing to see a local perform Mayella Ewell, the accuser. These two characters bring the show to its knees.

On a separate note, a book about Harper Lee *Furious Hours: Murder, Fraud, and The Last Trial of Harper Lee* is a fascinating true crime about Lee's extensive research into a case she ultimately abandons. She traveled with Truman Capote and helped him investigate what became *In Cold Blood*. I'm sure the *Furious Hours* case renewed her journalistic need to examine layers of evidence and find answers about insurance fraud via serial killing. The detective gene has deep roots as Lee studied law and began her writing career at her college newspaper. The alleged mastermind in *Furious Hours*, a black pastor, Willie Maxwell, collected multiple insurance settlements on members of his family. It is assumed Lee could have harmed the civil rights legacy that is *Mockingbird* if she published a nonfiction narrative of the Maxwell case. I wondered if *Furious Hours* was her attempt to make a mark in Capote's space? Or was this merely a home state case that fascinated her? Were Lee and Capote competitive and envious of one another? Truman was reportedly jealous of her *Mockingbird* fame from biographies I've read. His *Breakfast at Tiffany's* and *In Cold Blood* brought him fame, but nothing close to his Lee's literary stardom. It's hard to tell what became of their friendship once he scored his flock of swans in New York's social circles. FX's *FEUD: Capote Vs.*

The Swans based on Laurence Leamer's *Capote's Women* looks at the decline in his writing career and the betrayal of confidences he was entrusted with—which doesn't touch on his childhood friend, Lee.

Tickets to the show in Monroeville   *The outdoor portion of the set for Mockingbird*

Photos by Emily W. Skinner

Zorafest, Eatonville, Fl.—Zora Neale Hurston

Zora is the most famous black woman to hail from Florida next to Mary McLeod Bethune in my estimation. She was raised in Eatonville, Fl, one of the first self-governing black communities incorporated in the U.S. in 1887. And she's the most notable female author of the Harlem Renaissance from my searches. I've read her *Their Eyes Were Watching God* which was made into a film by Oprah Winfrey's Harpo Productions, along with her memoir *Dust Tracks on a Road,* as well as her newspaper coverage for the *Pittsburgh Courier* of the first trial of Ruby McCollum, a black woman accused of killing her Live Oaks, Florida lover (alleged lover), a white doctor and father of her son.

Orange County's Eatonville also hosts an annual Zora Festival that includes literature, music, art and food. If you want to learn more about the positive events that celebrate her legacy go to zorafestival.org. The year we attended Morris Day and The Time were headlining. As a Prince fan, I was thrilled that the festival included Morris Day. Still on my list is to pay respects to Zora at the cemetery where author Alice Walker worked to find Zora's originally unmarked grave and have it memorialized.

Hemingway House, Key West, Florida—Ernest Hemingway

Photo by Emily W. Skinner

We visited the Hemingway house when our kids were little and my brother stationed in Key West. Hemingway's home was the very first author landmark I had ever visited. The lore of the *Old Man and The Sea* and Hemingway's six-toed cat's feline descendants (that still live at the home) are what brought us there. Given my visit to Key West was more than twenty years ago, I looked up the landmark to learn it's still open to the public. There have been so many storms to hit Florida that I feared it might be in disrepair. https://www.hemingwayhome.com

Montgomery, Alabama—F. Scott and Zelda Fitzgerald Museum 6/29/2012

We visited the Fitzgerald Museum during a multi-stop road trip to Alpine and Birmingham, Alabama, as well as Tupelo and Walnut, Mississippi. F. Scott Fitzgerald's *The Great Gatsby* was one of my mentor's, Harry Whittington's favorite novels, and as such, Fitzgerald was on my radar. On our visit to the home Scott, Zelda and Scottie (their daughter) lived in for approximately six months, October 1931 to April 1932—we learned that director

Baz Luhrmann had bought the film rights to *Gatsby*. If I understood our guide correctly, Luhrmann paid one million for all rights (literary and film rights). That led me to believe that Luhrmann would also earn royalties on reprints of the book, but I can't find anything online that corroborates this. If I knew I'd be sharing this detail in a book, I would have written it down and confirmed I had it correct. Regardless, the museum has goodies that include ledgers handwritten by Fitzgerald detailing royalties, artwork by Zelda, and family artifacts. The landmark sign outside of the home says Fitzgerald was working on *Tender is the Night* and Zelda her memoir *Save Me The Waltz* while living there. At the time we were visiting only a portion of the house was utilized for the museum. Thank you, Montgomery, Alabama for giving literary buffs this intimate museum.

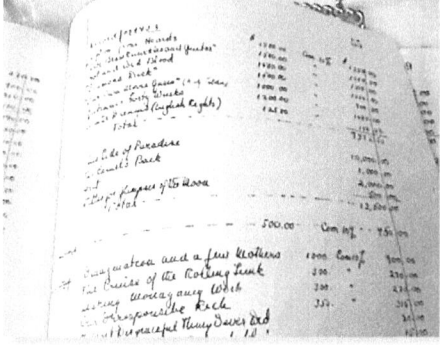

All Photos on this Page by Emily W. Skinner

Andalusia Farm, Milledgeville, Ga.—Flannery O' Connor home

As mentioned earlier, the trip to Milledgeville was twofold. Refer to the opening paragraphs of this chapter regarding the trip. A new film by Ethan Hawke, *Wildcat*, starring his daughter, Maya as Flannery O' Connor is a tad too weird as a representation of the Catholic author. If one is willing to read a biography about O'Connor, I recommend *Flannery: A Life of Flannery O' Connor*. The museum sells her books and this biography. If you read the aforementioned book, the *Wildcat* film's blend of author and characters might make better sense. Andalusia includes an interior walk through the home of her personal effects, as well as the farm buildings and the ground's resident animals, including Flannery's favorite fowl, peahens and peacocks. Definitely worth the trip. And stop by the Milledgeville Visitor's Center to learn about the infamous history of the asylum, Central State Hospital and consider a trolley tour of the hospital ruins (what exists—the state or city are now in the process of clearing much of the property). I believe the hospital inspired some of O'Connor's characters.

Me at Andalusia.
Photo by Tom Skinner

Rearview of the farm.
Photo by Emily W. Skinner

Margaret Mitchell House and Museum, Atlanta, Ga.

Margaret Mitchell was an Atlanta newspaper reporter who interviewed celebrities and wrote local features before writing her only novel, *Gone with the Wind*. *GWTW* is my favorite book and movie. My mother loved Clark Gable and this movie was a staple at our house when shown annually on television. I've read the book twice. The Civil War cast of Rhett, Scarlett and Ashley, I believe could easily be set in the first or second world war, or even outer space—and still maintain the sexual tension that is central to the story. Her youthful novella *Lost Laysen* provides insight into a love triangle that seems to be the inspiration for *Gone with the Wind*. The museum itself was an apartment building when Mitchell and her husband, John Marsh, lived there. Their small downstairs apartment (the lower left unit in the photo) fit forty guests standing when the couple entertained, and their

Exterior of Margaret Mitchell Museum. Photo by Emily W. Skinner

Margaret Mitchell's writing desk.

The bed Mitchell and Marsh shared was used as a buffet table when they entertained

bed a buffet table due to space restrictions our guide shared. This is the place where she wrote her bestseller while convalescing from a broken ankle. Marsh encouraged, edited and proofread his wife's bestseller. Her first husband, Red Upshaw, Red sounds like Rhett doesn't it, may have been the love of her life, but Marsh proved to be a dependable partner who would be by her side at her death. Mitchell was hit by a drunk driver in 1949 when she and Marsh were crossing a local street.

Marjorie Kinnan Rawlings Historic State Park, Cross Creek, Fl. The Yearling Restaurant, Hawthorne, Fl

Rawlings was a porch writer. This is her desk.   *This is the exterior of the home.*
Photos by Emily W. Skinner

Being a Floridian for the majority of my life, I had to learn more about Majorie Kinnan Rawlings. I remembered the movie *The Yearling* but had not read the book. So I picked up a first edition copy of her nonfiction book *Cross Creek*, a remembrance of living a backwoods lifestyle, looking forward to what made her the author she became. While I appreciated the strength she displays as a woman living a hammock existence alone, I was actually stunned by the racism in her retelling. She says in the book that she has been told she did good for the black people who worked on her property or were her nearby neighbors. She writes unapologetically. She was a tough woman and an educated author who was awarded acclaim for what I consider a bigoted account during this pre-Civil Rights period. I really don't know much more about Rawlings other than what I learned at her property (which was devoid of racism). I discovered through another source that Rawlings hosted Zora Neale Hurston in her home and was considered open-minded on race relations and would help anyone in need. I'm obviously judging her based on her own words in *Cross Creek*. She doesn't hide behind a veil in her autobiographical memoir about rural living. Studying authors sometimes bring unexpected results. An author's characters might be informed by their creator but ultimately each stands alone in history. Rawlings later moved out of the swamp to live a comfortable life and marry. She's not a native Floridian, but we claim her, as we do Hemingway, and Zora, who was born in Alabama, but resided in Florida throughout her lifetime.

The Yearling restaurant down the road from the state park serves home cooking and honors Rawling's beloved novel. While I hesitated to include Rawling in this section, I also feel I'm not willing to define a woman of accomplishment by the limitations of my knowledge. She told us who she was in my opinion. At times like this I look to MLK, Jr. for inspiration.

He said, "We must develop and maintain the capacity to forgive. He who is devoid of the power to forgive is devoid of the power to love. There is some good in the worst of us and some evil in the best of us. When we discover this, we are less prone to hate our enemies."

Concord, Mass—Orchard House—Louisa May Alcott

Louisa May Alcott's family home includes plenty of original pieces and notably the writing desk that her father made for her. The schoolhouse on the grounds was updated for Greta Gerwig's *Little Women* film and the back of Orchard House is a gift shop stocked with Alcott's novels. There I picked up a copy of *Louisa May Alcott: Her Life, Letters, and Journals* edited by Ednah Dow Cheney. These are my favorite reads. I love personal letter accounts that share period references and happenings. Not far from Orchard House is Sleepy Hollow Cemetery where Alcott and her peers are buried along with a wealth of Concord residents.

Me at Orchard House
Photo by Caitlin Poley

Top right: Inside home & School on the ground

Bottom right: Louisa's grave Author's Ridge.
Photos by Emily W. Skinner

Author's Ridge Cemetery at Sleepy Hollow—Emerson, Thoreau—Hawthorne—Alcott

Salem, Mass—The House of Seven Gables—Nathaniel Hawthorne

Hawthorne was such a cutie when he was younger—in this portrait. I image Louisa May Alcott developing a crush on him, as it appears she did with Emerson and Thoreau. Her letters and journal reveal she did go to Boston to write in solitude, and Salem is close by. I marvel at the community of literary talent in such close proximity. The House of Seven Gables Museum tour includes multiple buildings, one being the Nathaniel Hawthorne birthhome. The property was built in 1668 and has a *secret* passageway that I didn't believe was structurally possible to tour, given the age of the house. What a treat! Below are a few pictures. Down the road from the House of Seven Gables is the Salem Witch Museum. We toured both. https://7gables.org/

Nathaniel Hawthorne

The House of Seven Gables Museum

Museum Exterior. Photo by Emily W. Skinner

Paris, France—Victor Hugo Museum

Our trip to Paris in June 2024, was a dream come true. We made it to the Eiffel Tower, The Louvre, Napoleon's Chateau de Malmaison, Normandy, Monet's home, The Catacombs, the pyre of St. Joan of Arc, Dior museum and among my favorites was the Victor Hugo Museum. The museum is an apartment where he lived from 1832 to 1848. There is a courtyard café/coffee shop and small bookstore on site. The books are all published in French with the exception of one that discusses Hugo's sketches. I didn't know Hugo was a political figure until I visited the museum, which made perfect sense given the characters he writes about. This museum is free and definitely a Paris must!

Me at Victor Hugo Courtyard Café Photo by Tom Skinner

Photos of the Victor Hugo museum by Emily Skinner

Check out the writing desk on the right.

PART TWO

Harry Whittington

*Howard and Lot Whittington at Regal Cinema in Largo, when we all went to see The Great Gatsby, Harry's favorite book.
Photo by Emily W. Skinner*

I Need To Let Harry Go

I published a short nonfiction memoir a few years ago titled *Master of the Roman Noir* (you'll find it in this section) to honor my mentor Harry Whittington after he passed away. I originally interviewed him for a newspaper article (also in this section) and thought I had lost the piece but found it thirty-five years later. My husband often says I need to let Harry go. The reason being, I usually introduce Harry before I introduce myself when talking to readers. I give credit where credit is due. Harry taught me A LOT about writing novels in a very short window of time. As such, I have shared my appreciation for Harry on social media and blog posts. Nonetheless Harry's still unknown to many, with the exception of pulp novel and western enthusiasts. Producers and directors who have found me online, email me for a contact to Harry's estate to option his novels for film. If you had Googled Harry Whittington up to 2005, you'd get articles about his pulp novels. Then in February of 2006 former Vice President, Dick Cheney, shot his friend Harry Whittington who survived (no relation to the author) and now that comes up in searches ahead of Harry Whittington the author. Though Harry's estate bought the domain www.harrywhittington.com in recent years (which is a blank page as of this writing), his site doesn't even come up in a name search.

After Harry died in 1989, I visited Kathryn Whittington, Harry's wife, with some regularity. Years would pass and Howard Whittington, Harry and Kathryn's son, would hire a woman to help Kathryn. Howard and Lot (Kathryn's caregiver) eventually fell in love and married. Kathryn died August of 2005. My husband Tom and I would connect with Howard and Lot around 2011 to reminisce about his parents and build an ongoing friendship.

A little backstory on Howard, he was a Pinellas County Judge who stepped down because he didn't like putting men in jail for back child support when he felt the offender's wages could be garnished if the man continued to work versus sit in jail. That's how he explained it to us. The judicial hierarchy had expectations for judges to incarcerate a good number of deadbeat dads. Harry and Kathryn were very proud of their son, the judge. Afterall, it was Harry's writing royalties that put Howard through law school, so it seemed the transition back to private practice was not an easy decision for Howard.

When Harry passed away, Howard managed his father's estate and was always hopeful his father's vast backlist would produce more film options. Howard's sister Harriet, I didn't know well. She was a daddy's girl by all appearances in the best loving way. I saw her a few times at the Whittington home and at Harry's funeral. Harriet had a beautiful smile and bubbly personality like her mother. When Howard was five years old, he said he was convinced Harriet was out to get him. In his recollection, in 1947 Harriet left him to fend for himself for several hours at Webb City (a shopping destination dubbed the *World's Most Unusual Drug Store* in St. Petersburg from 1926 to 1979 that no longer exists) as she ran off with her friends. He was five and she was ten. Harriet finally came back for him and took him home to their 20th St. S. residence in St. Petersburg—and he never forgot the experience. He also said she put straight pins in his bed (one time) to torment him. That was the extent of the horror or mean sister stories. He'd laugh about it, then get serious and say, "I think she wanted to kill me."

During our dinners, Howard would share random updates about anything JET Literary (who represented film and literary rights at the time) might option or republish. It always seemed something was on the horizon but not moving with urgency. As I reread my original interview with Harry while writing this memoir, a thought jumped out at me. As such, I wanted to see if it was possible to still reach Jim or Liz Trupin. Both graciously responded. I had met the Trupins (the agent owners of JET—J for Jim, E for Elizabeth, T for Trupin Literary) at one of Harry's gatherings in the 1980s. At some point the Trupins divorced and divided JET under a new arrangement. Jim handled foreign language and film rights and lived overseas. Liz handled everything domestically according to Howard and remained in the United States. It appears JET is much the same today. I'll get back to the Trupins.

Among those who also represented Harry was Donald MacCampbell from 1955 to 1962. I discovered a MacCampbell lawsuit (on courthouse records) when I went looking for where Harry and Kathryn resided in Pinellas County using courthouse records, as well as genealogy tools. Harry, I discovered, brought legal action against MacCampbell April 2, 1962, in an Affidavit filed at Pinellas County Courthouse with a *Safety Harbor Herald* legal notice published March 2, 9, 16, 23, 1962 stating that Harry was seeking a … *rescission of a contract between plaintiff and defendant.* On July 3, 1962, a Domestic Relations Judgement was filed that wasn't viewable on the county website. So, I contacted the Pinellas County Courthouse and received a copy of the Final Decree that, "immediately rescinded, abrogated and undone from the beginning and all rights of defendant, Donald MacCampbell, to continue to function further as agent of plaintiff, Harry Whittington…" I will spare the entire legal language.

Then I realized that MacCampbell must be the unnamed agent Harry mentioned in his *I Remember It Well* foreword of a Black Lizard release in 1987 (when JET Literary represented him). Harry said his agent (I'll presume MacCampbell) wanted him to write nonfiction and rejected five novels he'd sent him that year. Harry wrote five novels that MacCampbell wasn't willing to pitch to publishers.—Harry then turned around and sold the five novels on his own. MacCampbell must have found out and felt he was entitled to 10% commission of the five book sales. That's when Harry took him to court. And interestingly enough, MacCampbell doesn't name Harry in his memoir. But MacCampbell does say he was "bombarding" the nonfiction markets in 1961 with political books by established authors and would be authors he was developing on Capitol Hill. I surmise this is why MacCampbell didn't want to spend time selling Harry's five fiction novels when he could push a prolific author to perhaps pump out five nonfiction titles quickly?

And as luck would have it, Jim Trupin explained in email communication that, "He (Harry) was at one point repped by this guy who told me over a tedious lunch that he was known as Mr. Paperback (the agent). His first name might've been Don (Are you thinking what I'm thinking? *Donald* MacCampbell mentioned in the lawsuit above). "Anyway, I've erased this guy from my memory," Trupin said.

I searched for MacCampbell online and married up the term Trupin used Mr. Paperback to Mr. Pocket Books mentioned on the dust jacket of MacCampbell's autobiographical memoir of agenting *Don't Step On It-It Might Be A Writer*, published 1972.

The inside back jacket flap reads, "By the early 1950's *Writer's Digest* was calling him (MacDonald) "Mr. Pocket Books" on the strength of his fortified position in the paperback field, while the Attorney General's office was looking into complaints that he was running a monopoly." So maybe Harry wasn't the only one who had a problem with MacCampbell?

Trupin shared that, "We were recommended to Harry by one of our other writers, Will Knott. I believe he (Harry) was long gone from his job at the Department of Agriculture." I'm getting to a point. Stay with me.

In *I Remember It Well* Harry said that in 1975 Anita Diamant represented him thanks to his wife's instigation and there began his pseudonym, Ashley Carter. He also had a Hollywood agent Mauri Grashin along the way who was also a screenwriter. Diamant would be part of Harry's second act, after leaving his government job in Washington, D.C., which is the Department of Agriculture job Trupin mentions. Harry was an editor for the Rural Electrification Administration at the U.S. Department of Agriculture. As a side note I have to share a new detail I just learned from Harry's July 5th, 1988, NPR interview with Terry Gross of *Fresh Air,* from the WUSF Studio in Tampa, "When I got there (Rural Electrification Administration), they were having trouble at these meetings they were having all over the country. They were so dull. The government speakers would come in and they would put people to sleep. And people weren't arriving early for the meeting. So they decided that they would put on a play, an act each day over three days to get people there early. So they had me write and direct it. And it made such a hit that for the next seven years that's about all I did."

Regarding my hunch, recollecting my interview with Harry, he told me he quit writing between 1968 through 1975 because he felt he was all washed up.

Why was Harry so discouraged?

Oddly, it was because of a bestseller titled, *The Man From U.N.C.L.E* "The Doomsday Affair."

Harry stated during our 1982 interview that "The Doomsday Affair," was a turning point. A true *doomsday* to him, my words, not his. Which led me to believe he was two different authors. The revelation I called a hunch earlier really plagued me.

1. The author who risked a secure government paycheck (quitting the post office) to become a working writer selling short stories, pulp novels and screenplays hoping <u>to transition to the literary leagues</u> of F. Scott Fitzgerald, Ernest Hemingway, John Steinbeck, William Faulkner, and Erskine Caldwell.

2. The author who stopped writing <u>when his literary dream moved further out of reach</u>, only to return to a government job for the security of a paycheck. But ultimately, he couldn't stay away from writing novels.

The two Harrys had paycheck issues.

- <u>Harry Number 1</u>—lived the dream 1944 to 1967 as a working author to prove he could make a career of writing, in spite of the odds.
- <u>Harry Number 2</u>—would come back to write in 1975, accepting his literary aspirations were not likely to materialize, but recognized he could continue to earn a living writing or working for the government. The choice was his.

But really, he was the same Harry all along, who I believe longed for an agent or representative to stop him from genre writing and push him to try his hand at a literary novel. Harry said as much in the French fanzine *Les Amis Du Crime,* March 1980, "I didn't write anything between 1968 and 1975 because I was very disjointed, enraged by my literary career." Technically, he didn't have a literary career. He was a successful author in multiple genres, but not specifically literary novels.

Surpassing many authors he competed with by sheer volume, Harry's bibliography (depending on the source) ranges from 170 to 200 total novels in a variety of genres. In my unscholarly opinion, literary novelists during his and their lifetimes, Fitzgerald was his idol, so I am including him, averaged under forty novels.

I looked at the literary output and bibliographies by date range of authors (sources in the back of this book) I believed were a match to Harry's sensibilities and characterization for the same period. Fitzgerald (Five novels from 1920-1939), Hemingway (Ten novels from 1926-1986), Steinbeck (Twenty-nine books 1937-1952), Faulkner (Nineteen 1926-1962), Caldwell (Twenty-Five 1929-1987). All authored short stories, as did Harry, but Harry wrote more than all of these established literary giants combined. He was in a league of his own. Of his pulp peers he wrote more novels than many of them individually: Raymond Chandler (Seven novels 1939-1958), Gil Brewer (Eighteen 1951-1967), Talmage Powell (Seven 1942-1971), Paul Cain (One 1932), and John D. MacDonald (Seventy books 1950-1984).

In *I Remember It Well* Harry says, "The reason why I wrote and sold more than almost everyone else was that I was living on the edge of ruin, and I was naïve."

And Harry might have also been naïve expecting his representatives and publishers to recognize his literary potential. After all he said it in *I Remember It Well,* "Since I wanted only to be Scott Fitzgerald, with a touch of sardonic Maugham, and J.P. McEvoy humor…"

213

And once his work started selling, he said, "I was less than a household name, but I was too busy, and having too much fun, to care."

So busy, I think even he lost track of his literary goal, until *Doomsday*.

Le Monde, 1957, Paris newspaper wrote, "With this novel, FRENZIE PASTORALE (*Desire in The Dust*), which compares favorably with Erskine Caldwell's best, Whittington asserts himself as one of the greats among American novelists." That was 1957!

As late as 1980 French critic Jean-Jacques Schleret reiterates, "*DESIRE IN THE DUST* is one of your most ambitious novels, written in the style of (William) Faulkner and Erskine Caldwell..."

Harry responded to Schleret, "This is one (*Desire in The Dust*) of my favorite Southern novels. It was first purchased by Fabio Jegher from Paris to be filmed in France. I think the script he prepared was much superior to the film distributed by 20th Century Fox, after Jegher had sold the rights. I always wondered what this story would have looked like in a French film." Harry wasn't fond of the American version starring Raymond Burr, Ken Scott, Martha Hyer and Joan Bennett.

So, if critics were comparing his work to southern literary giants Faulkner and Caldwell, why didn't his agents pitch his literary potential?

In a *Los Angeles Times* April 13, 1987, article "Erskine Caldwell, Author of 'God's Little Acre,' 'Tobacco Road,' Dies," by Jack Jones reads, "God's Little Acre," banned in Boston and reviled by many after it was published in 1933, was at one time the champion best-seller with more than 10 million copies. Last year it was still 10th on the all-time fiction list." Caldwell's obit is an amazing testament to legacy writing that stands the test of time.

If Erskine Caldwell sold 10 million copies, perhaps Harry could have, too. But he didn't have a chance to come up for air as he was writing as fast as he could to stay ahead of creditors. It also didn't help that Harry spent a lot of money making a movie that never got distributed, *The Face of the Phantom*. But the point is, no one recognized a gold mine opportunity by all indications. It's one thing to know you have great ideas and another to have someone say, "Stop whatever you're doing and write the book that only you can write."

His buddy Gil Brewer attempted to say as much in the note that I found posted on Twitter. See the image below.

So why did a television tie-in book, *The Man from U.N.C.L.E.*, "The Doomsday Affair" push him over the edge?

Harry was a pulp author, then a paperback original author. Pulps would qualify as novellas for their word count under 40,000 words. Novels range from 40,000 words plus. Pulps followed genre categories like hard-boiled detective, nurse romances and such. A paperback original was printed on heavier paper stock and could have the same qualities as a literary novel, though the initial release would only be in paperback, no hardcover edition.

Genre novels today can have hardcover releases and not qualify as a literary novel. A literary agent earns more for their clients by first releasing in hardcover, followed by a softcover. Today an ebook book or audiobook will be included. Harry had some early hardcover releases, his first book, *Vengeance Valley*, 1945, a western and his second novel *Her Sin*, 1946, a trashy crime tale both by Phoenix Press. Hardcover releases for the most part established an author with distinction that set them apart from genre authors, or the early pulp writer. Long ago hardcover books were collected by the wealthy who built personal libraries. When the pulps arrived, the world opened up for everyone.

A literary novel, according to *Writer's Digest* magazine, is not considered to be a plot driven work or even fast paced. There's room to wander in a literary setting. There's a possibility of inner dialogue or struggle that may build or doesn't. It might be amusing, miserable, or even ethereal. And the conclusion might possibly land softly or with a hard examination of the conscience or be left open-ended. In my own definition, the literary novel is a lot like life. There are characters we meet that we may not understand, who do things that make no sense or may well provide wisdom. They fill up space and time in our lives leaving us feeling warm or scratching our heads and are nevertheless unforgettable. In Harry's case, F. Scott Fitzgerald's Jay Gatsby captured him. Captured him in a way that made Harry want to follow Fitzgerald as a writer and ultimately dream of a Gatsby existence. But Harry needed an advocate to help him find his way out of the labyrinth of genre plots that kept him in the swamps, Florida orange groves, southern plantations and old west towns. Of his protagonist, Harry said in an interview with *Les Amis Du Crime*, March 1980: "I hope that the reader will, with me, want to see him triumph over the impossible situations in which he finds himself." Write what you know.

But circling back to the point Harry made, he was discouraged by his literary career after 24 years of toil. In the 1988 NPR interview with Terry Gross, timed perfectly with the Black Lizard releases, she hit on my argument at the end of the interview. She said it differently, but she points to his missed opportunity. "You're a very good writer, don't you feel you're wasting your talents writing Mandingo novels?" In 1988 Harry was still writing *Falconhurst/Mandingo* novels as Ashley Carter. He noted the books paid very well and humbly replied, "I don't feel I'm wasting my talents writing anything. I'll tell you why. I have had to do the very best I could do on everything I wrote. Everything I wrote I had to do the best I could do, because there wasn't any other way I could sell it. I didn't know anybody. I actually didn't have any friends among publishers or anything like that. I just had to do the best I could."

Harry didn't have a Maxwell Perkins, the book editor for Charles Scribner's Sons, who discovered F. Scott Fitzgerald and Ernest Hemingway and even had a hand in Erskine Caldwell's beginnings. Harry had agents who found him good opportunities but perhaps lacked vision.

"There's no magic formula for building a writer other than having the publishing process click for all parties," Trupin said. "There has to be a consistency in the quality and imagination in the story line and the ability to deliver a manuscript in a timely manner."

In referencing *The Man From U.N.C.L.E.* series, Trupin shared, "It's been about 40 years since Harry and I spoke or that we repped any of his works so I can only offer modest help/recollections of him and his work. So, bits and pieces. I can't speak to anything relating to *U.N.C.L.E.*, have no idea who repped it. As for tie-ins, they were normally flat fee although there were exceptions. I did a deal for one of my writers to ghost a series… which had a small royalty attached, maybe 2%. It went to No. 1 on the NYT (*New York Times Best Sellers* list). So, the renewal advance was seven figures to make up for the absence of a royalty. A wash, in the end since the sales started to peter out from their initial level."

Did you understand that? I'm not really sure I do, other than tie-in books are normally a flat fee, with exceptions. Wouldn't Harry be the exception with his level of experience? I think Harry might have been fine if his flat fee tie-in had publishers knocking down his door for more bestseller material that included a healthy advance, especially a literary opportunity.

In an article published in the Tampa Tribune March 12, 1978, by Ed Hirschberg, an English professor at the University of South

Florida, regarding Harry's hiatus from writing, Hirschberg said, "He (Harry) tried it (quitting), for good, about 10 years ago, when he got disgusted with his agent for failing to make adequate provision for his royalties on the publication of the book based on the popular TV series *The Man from U.N.C.L.E.* The book happened to be hugely successful "Doomsday Affair," which topped the paperback bestseller lists for a whole year—but all Whittington ever got out of it was $1,500. The royalties would have amounted to at least 10 times more than that."

A surprising twist of fate came in Harry's comeback. When I interviewed Harry in 1982, he and Kathryn lived in a two-story waterfront home on the intercoastal waterway of Harbor Drive in Indian Rocks Beach. Harry told me the house was an affirmation he'd made it. Perhaps this was as close as he'd get to a West Egg mansion the likes of Jay Gatsby? Not as opulent as the trappings of the Jazz age protagonist, Harry's Harbor Drive home was a reward paid for by his laboring over manual typewriters and later word processing machines for the majority of his life. Harry surpassed Fitzgerald in determination and volume.

Jim Trupin, "When we (he and his wife Liz) met Harry, he and Kathryn were living in a small house (on 1st Avenue N, Indian Rocks Beach) with his mother, Granny, in an even smaller house maybe fifty yards away." I had heard Kathryn talk about a little house they kept as a rental while living on Harbor Drive. So, I wanted to patch together how their lives progressed to the Harbor Drive victory. In my exploration I learned that they purchased the Harbor Drive home on November 3, 1981 (from Pinellas County Courthouse records). Harry would've been 66 at the time. Trupin explained, "I do remember one of the contracts we got for him enabled him to buy the larger house (on Harbor Drive) in IRB. We also visited a couple of times to watch the *Super Bowl* on that enormous screen he'd installed and which covered an entire wall."

The house was made possible by opportunities JET Literary provided. The television was a rear projection which was popular at the time. Harry, a film buff, had the closest thing to a home theater that existed then. But going back to the home where the Whittingtons lived when the Trupins first met them, Howard Whittington shared the home on 1st Avenue was built with a side door versus a front door per Harry's specifications. "Who does that?" Howard said. I originally thought Howard was implying something covert, like Harry was hiding from someone or something, a trait a Whittington character would definitely possess. *Write what you know.* But as it turned out, Howard meant Harry wanted no distractions. His home was a private residence and as such, no solicitors allowed. No interruptions to his writing.

But if we were to map the road to Harry's final destination, it would begin in Ocala, Florida 1915. A rural community where his father was a grocer. A very unsuccessful grocer at times, Howard related. Harry Sr. would not feed his family from his limited inventory. I found an article "Remembering Our Region's Bestselling Author" written by Joshua Braley for *The Gainesville Sun*. He attempted to track Harry's life and reported, "… take State Highway 19 west, into the heart of the Ocala National Forest. Whittington's family lived on a farm in this area during his boyhood, and it supplies the setting for his most atmospheric Florida fiction."

Harry and parents and siblings would move to St. Petersburg and Harry attend St. Petersburg High School but he actually graduated from Ocala High School. He's listed in the 1930 St. Petersburg High School yearbook where he would eventually meet Kathryn Odom, his future wife. Braley reported that Whittington,

"… worked at the old open-air Post Office at 76 Fourth Street North (in St. Petersburg)."

Harry B. Whittington, Sr. and Rosa Whittington, Harry's parents, along with Harry, his sister Rosa, and brother Charles, by census accounts lived on Queen St. S., in St. Petersburg which is now a vacant lot. The home Harry and Kathryn would later live at on 20th St. S. is still there. Another address on 21st St S. in St. Petersburg is also a vacant lot.

Their three homes on Indian Rocks Beach are all still standing, though Hurricanes Helene and Milton brought damage to the Harbor Drive home I learned from the current owner. The two side-by-side properties on 1st Avenue N, (the one without a front entrance) is now gaining a 2nd floor addition. The little house looks untouched though I haven't inquired if the interior was damaged. As you can see from my Author Haunts chapter, I like to know where authors lived and worked.

In pursuing the Trupins to resolve my theory on "The Doomsday Affair," I asked if Harry ever questioned contracts after receiving the flat fee from "The Doomsday Affair"? Again, the Trupins were not Harry's agent at this juncture, but it made me wonder if Harry paid closer attention to their contracts, after such a stinging loss of royalties. "Harry never questioned contracts," Jim Trupin said, "He just signed them."

As for Harry's estate it was managed by Howard with the input of Kathryn and Harriet. It is now in the care of Harriet's daughter, Suzy. Harriet, I learned at her funeral in 2017, formed a friendship with author Rick Ollerman, who eventually bought her North Florida home. He was interested in writing about Harry and working with Harriet.

David Laurence Wilson, another author, approached Howard years earlier to help with rereleasing many Whittington titles.

Ollerman and Wilson were uniquely aligned with one of Harry and Kathryn's offspring. Both have written for Stark House Press which has released newer versions of Harry's novels. Wilson also penned several introductions that speak to Harry's career, as well as Harry's lost 38 or 39 books. Wilson shared Harry was represented by the Scott Meredith agency as it relates to the lost books. But perhaps, the agency actually repped the banker who ordered the books from Harry. More on that below. The origins of the lost books differ from Ollerman to Wilson.

In the Stark House Noir Classics edition *To Find Cora, Like Mink Like Murder* and *Body and Passion,* Wilson details his activities working with Howard Whittington, including his process in finding the lost Whittington titles. These nineteen pages of Whittington history are attributed to named sources and provide the reader a comprehensive short biography of Harry Whittington.

Howard Whittington shared that the lost books were part of an arrangement Harry made with a banker in St. Petersburg. In *I Remember It Well* Harry said, "I signed, in 1964, to do a 60,000-word novel a month for a publisher under his house names. I was paid $1,000 on the first of each month. I wrote one of these novels each month for 39 months." Howard explained that Harry ghostwrote books for the banker who wanted to embellish and publish them under his (the banker's) own pseudonym. The banker owned the stories having paid Harry some much-needed cash. The books were intended for adult book racks and not 100% Whittington. Harry didn't want to be associated with them. But it is interesting that he does admit to writing 39 books in 39 months. It cost him three years of his life, so it's understandable he'd want to have some account for that much of his writing existence. Ollerman also had a similar take on this (perhaps) as shared to him by Harriet. And it seems reasonable that if Harry was only writing these to pay off debt, that Wilson's detective work to find the books and pseudonyms—as the publisher would have worked with the banker, not Harry, a serious challenge.

In Wilson's introduction for the Stark House reprint of *A Night For Screaming* and *Any Woman He Wanted*, Wilson gave a very well-rounded biographical sketch of Harry's life. A cradle-to-grave telling with references on milestone data and quotes. With Wilson's access to documents and files working directly with Howard Whittington, it would be helpful if he updated the introduction of Stark House's release of *Rapture Alley, Winter Girl, and Strictly For The Boys*. As a fan, I would like the Wilson sources of some of the published quotes and the period. An example of an innocent enough Wilson error. Wilson writes in the edition, "His (Harry's) monument is there along Florida's Gulf Coast, a tribute on a gravestone: "The King of the Paperbacks." However, Harry's grave marker actually reads, "Master of the Roman Noir" "One of the Greats Among American Novelists." Sounds picky I know, but it would have been better to say he was paraphrasing or mention who quoted the gravestone label to him.

On Harriet's side of the equation, Ollerman explained in email correspondence with me that he hoped to someday produce a Harry Whittington biography from interviews he conducted with Harriet and Howard. He, too, had access to records via Harriet, to help her in organizing Harry's history which were returned to Harriet's daughter, Suzy, when the estate hired their current representation, AKA Literary for literary rights and William Morris Agency for film rights. Maybe Greg Shephard, publisher of Stark House Press, who works with Ollerman and Wilson individually, could bring them together for a two-part Whittington biography from their own unique perspective. I would buy it!

I Need To Let Harry Go

At present limited reprints of Harry's novels are published by Stark House Press. Used books can be found on Amazon and by treasure hunting used book retailers. Stark House's ebook of Harry's *A Ticket to Hell* and *Hell Can Wait* includes an investigation by former FBI agent Tom Simon, who walks through Harry's past in a clinical way. Just the facts. I didn't find much new in Simon's travels from Harry's birthplace in Ocala to his move to St. Petersburg, Florida where his novel writing career began in 1944—but sincerely appreciated his clever breakdown of Harry's life from an evidentiary approach.

And with Harry, Kathryn, Harriet, and now Howard (he died in 2023) all gone, Suzy, Harriet's daughter, Harry's granddaughter, is the glue that keeps Harry's legacy intact. Suzy is truly an amazing businesswoman. I appreciate her friendship. Her daughter Ryann Cantrell is the only descendant (by all appearances) who has an interest in becoming a novelist. So, I'm keeping my fingers crossed for a future release. She's definitely got a great grandfatherly angel to watch over her.

As far as the film people who have contacted me along the way, I am hopeful for some Harry Whittington releases in the near future. One being Travis Mills' *Frontier Crucible,* a western in post-production (at this time) Mills adapted from Harry's *Desert Stake-Out*. Mills boasts he followed the book exactly. That would make Harry very happy! As well I am very grateful for a friendship I've developed with film producer Arthur Goldblatt who has been working to bring a few Whittington titles to life.

But as far as my letting Harry go, I'm not sure that's possible.

> For Harry and Kathryn:
>
> Harry, if you don't sit yourself down and write the honest to God book of your guts very soon, I'm sure as hell going to bash you over the head with a sledge hammer.
>
> I mean it.

A Photo Posted On Twitter
Written by author Gil Brewer to Harry (and Kathryn)
Source lost.

Public domain photo related to Harry's directorial debut, The Face of The Phantom.

Master of the *Roman Noir*

All Rights Reserved Copyright 2016
by Emily W. Skinner

Howard Whittington, Ann (Howard's friend), me, Harry Whittington
Photo taken by Kathryn Whittington

Harry Whittington was—as he still is—one of Florida's best kept secrets. So much so that it has always been my desire to get him on the state map along with Marjorie Kinnan Rawlings, Ernest Hemingway and Zora Neale Hurston. Many of his novels were made into movies or television series, including Lawman, Dakotas, Charro and more. Most of his pseudonyms were variations of his name or his family members, and the two genres he is most noted for are pulp detective and westerns, though he wrote romances too.

Harry and his wife, Kathryn, were residents of Indian Rocks Beach, Florida when we met. Though he passed away June 11, 1989, I still miss him today and share his story to any listening ear.

I remember little about arranging our feature story interview, but what I do remember is sitting on the back patio of his house overlooking the intra-coastal waterway. The Whittingtons lived right on the water and Harry loved that house. It was a landmark homestead to him—he had finally arrived, even if it had taken a lifetime.

Harry grew up dirt poor in Ocala, Florida. So, poor that as a kid he vividly remembered the neighbors feeding his younger brother while he watched from outside the window.

Everyone in Ocala was poor during the Great Depression. And as such the rural community helped each other as best they could with what they could… and Harry never forgot that it didn't include him!

I don't say this to make him sound bitter, but it was that pain that made him the writer of gutsy, downtrodden protagonists. Harry knew what it was like to go hungry and to watch from the sidelines.

For Harry, the house on the intercoastal gave him a feeling of accomplishment after years of toil as an underpaid writer who churned out books that sold well in multiple genres, and many were made into television series and movies. However, he didn't make money in proportion to the effort he put out. He wasn't ungrateful, but he admitted he was naive. He had some good years financially, and many more as a recognized master, but the rewards, even today, are still off balance. Harry is still in the shadows of his pulp peers.

During our afternoon interview, white herons flew in and hung out. Kathryn, the love of Harry's life, fed them hotdogs, an obvious routine. I had never known birds to eat meat and was fascinated. Kathryn laughed a lot, apologizing for her disruptive feathered friends. She loved the birds and to brag about all things Harry. She didn't want anyone to miss a detail.

Harry sat in the shade of the greenery, and I just marveled at his story. I barely had to ask a question. Harry loved to talk about writing and his favorite author, F. Scott Fitzgerald. He fondly called him Scott Fitzgerald. You'd think they were great friends the way Harry spoke of his idol. I personally believe Harry most identified with the mysterious Jay Gatsby. Harry never enjoyed the wealth of Gatsby nor the fame of Fitzgerald, but he gave the world what these men couldn't. A body of work.

Harry also loved FDR, and what the Roosevelt administration gave the world. In Harry's eyes the pulps or mass market paperbacks (in large part funded by the Federal Writer's Project during the Great Depression) gave the world an affordable book at .25 to .35 cents a copy.

When the world was poor, Harry explained to me, Roosevelt's Works Progress Administration funded writers (and the arts) making it affordable for the masses to buy books that weren't as expensive hard cover novels.

I'll admit, I don't know the dynamics of how the FWP worked, but this is the interpretation I recall from Harry. The funding went to the publishers, who could then hire writers to produce stories as paperback originals vs. hard cover books. So, by creating the paperback industry, the world could read more, enjoy literature and more writers could have careers.

During our afternoon together, Harry took me through his life history and the gutsy move he made to quit a good job at the post office after being in the military and become a writer. The decision forced him to produce some 200 novels (over his lifetime and the number is still debated given his many pseudonyms) at a record pace. After all, he had a son, daughter and wife to feed.

While many of us wouldn't sacrifice a good government job and risk failure or going hungry to take a chance on a dream, Harry wasn't going to let anything stop him. I believe he still feared hunger, but he wasn't going to let the beast keep him from being a working author. He survived the Great Depression; he'd go mad writing before he'd let the beast win.

Harry had the naive courage to just do it! Most of us would have kept the post office job and tried to fit writing in where possible. In his words, "I came to writing from a love of words."

Harry, like many of his characters, lived on the edge. He had creditors and editors on his back for every written word he could produce. He thrived in that space.

Harry was not only a rival of Day Keene, Gil Brewer and Raymond Chandler, but he was also a rival of Louis L'Amour when he wrote westerns. He was a master of fiction. No genre could contain him.

Once he learned to plot (which took 13 years) the doors opened. The universe was his.

Harry told me that several of the Florida pulp novelists would get together and, while in each other's homes, they would add a sentence to whatever was in the host's typewriter. This, of course, had to be incorporated into the storyline. He was referring specifically to a visit at John D. MacDonald's.

As a new writer, I was in awe of his talent, history and generous nature.

Once my interview was published in the beach papers, I cautiously waited to get back in touch with Harry. I was afraid to bother him.

Where do we get these ideas about bothering people? I waited a few months.

When I did reach Harry, he was happy to hear from me and wanted more copies of the paper. He loved the article! In fact, he sent it to his publisher and I was overjoyed, but also unable to get more back issues.

Sadly, I still can't find that article in my clips. **(Update: I found the article. See subsequent pages)** I was so insecure about my writing and Harry's legacy that I wasn't sure I wrote something worthy of him. I kept one paper from every edition during that period, but Harry's is still missing.

But the happier news is we went on to become friends. Still timid, I was willing to put myself out there. Harry was a Board Member of the Suncoast Writer's Conference and I attended for many years.

I was an observer at social events Harry and Kathryn hosted when his publisher and other writers were in attendance. As a local feature writer, I just felt out of place with novelists. I adored them and their world but didn't feel comfortable.

When I met my future husband Tom, I was still working for the beach papers and later moved up to the Clearwater Sun daily newspaper as an entertainment reporter. Harry and Kathryn came to our wedding. Our wedding gift from the Whittington's was a glass pie dish and case. I still have it. Kathryn likely selected it, but it still seemed symbolic of the hungry writer and his family who lived on advances and royalty checks.

Once Tom and I married, we were immersed in a new life and its ups and downs. Two years went by and along came our first daughter, Marquel. I lost track of Harry and Kathryn during these years, I regret. I'd call or send a Christmas card. They were only a few miles away, but as a young couple, we were struggling with finances. I was still writing for the papers and starting to waitress on the side to make ends meet.

I was somewhat in Harry-mode myself at the time, trying to make a living as a writer and earn enough. I didn't even get the connection until recently!

But instead of writing novels, I was writing features and chasing Milton Berle, Jay Leno, Melissa Manchester and whoever was coming into town. I had regular freelance checks coming in and I was a working writer.

Not long after Marquel arrived, I lost my spot as a stringer for the Sun. The editor wanted the staff writers to write the news and stringers weren't needed. The paper was struggling.

During the years that followed I worked data entry at a few investment banking firms and we later opened a children's and maternity wear store and I focused on being a mom.

I stopped writing.

A few more years passed, it started to eat me up. I wanted to write and couldn't get my mojo. And it struck me. I hadn't talked with Harry in years!

I called Harry and said I wanted to come over and visit. He was happy to hear from me and it was like synchronicity. I couldn't believe it. We were picking up where we left off and I was uplifted. It was fate.

When I saw Harry, he looked a little worn, but had the same happy spirit I knew. He invited me over and while we were chatting, he said he may need me...

I couldn't figure out why he would need me? I needed him!

He said he was sick and needed to wrap up a Hawaiian novel in a series he was writing. He was about halfway through the project and wanted me to help him finish it so he could send it to his agent.

Me? I suddenly felt sick. I actually wanted to vomit. I would have rather helped Scarlett deliver Melanie's baby than hear this.

Just as Scarlett slapped Prissy in *Gone with the Wind* for saying she "didn't know nothin' about birthin babies," I was slapped by this moment and Harry's words. I wanted to run away, too.

I didn't know nothin' about writin' novels!

But instead of running, I left with a box that contained an outline and the portion of the book Harry had written. My assignment was to bring back the next chapter for his review in a few days.

Harry wrote a chapter a day. That's how he worked.

Oh my God!

That is all I could think. He is a rocket scientist and I'm the kid who rides her bicycle around the neighborhood and wants to be a rocket scientist. Yet now, the rocket scientist has sent me home with a rocket kit that he needs me to finish, so he can send it to NASA right away.

During these days we had many long discussions about writing, his family and how he wanted to be remembered. I personally never thought much about why he was sharing this with me. I just thought we were growing our friendship, and I was getting my mojo.

I also learned plotting and his work routine. He wouldn't let up on me, which was good.

The first attempts at chapter writing were a major disappointment to him. He didn't say it, but he had a look of exasperation. It was so awkward to tax a sick man with my inability.

Every few days I was back with a chapter and one day he proclaimed, "You can do this!" I finally got the hang of it. But it really didn't last long. He knew what he wanted and while I was learning to write books, I couldn't really write what he needed. It made me sad.

At the same time, he was feeling worse.

I don't know where it was in this writing process, but I ran my novel idea by him.

I had an *aha* moment during the course of our work together and the character *Marquel* came to life. I was very excited to share this with him, but not to distract from what we were doing. He asked me to write an outline, as I had learned his process, and also bring a sample chapter for him to read.

Harry was a man who didn't show weakness or ever want to show weakness. As the days progressed, I would await him in his writing room/office and a few times he was in pajamas. I knew he wasn't well, and I could hear rumblings from his stomach and he fought to keep up with what he was doing.

At some abrupt point, we stopped. Harry worked on the book as he was able and I stopped coming by. Weeks after Harry suffered a stroke and Kathryn called me.

I went to the hospital to see Harry and he had the obvious signs of a stroke and couldn't speak. He did motion to me. He was trying to tell me something.

Now I must admit, I was extremely emotional at this point and his family was there and I had always had a fear of death. So, I wasn't certain if Harry would improve.

I said to Kathryn, "I don't understand what Harry wants me to do."

He was still motioning. She said, "He wants you to know he likes what you gave him. Your book."

Harry seemed to agree from what I could tell, and I felt this overwhelming joy.

That was the last time I saw him.

Harry passed away shortly after, I don't recall if it was days or weeks, but it wasn't long.

When I got the news, I was struck by all the information he shared with me about how he wanted to be remembered.

To pay tribute, I brought a cherished antique typewriter to a florist to make a funeral arrangement. I had it filled with flowers and I inserted my goodbye letter.

When I arrived at the funeral home, the typewriter was in the entry to greet those coming to pay their respects.

Mission accomplished! Harry would be so happy. I was so grateful to have had the divine inspiration to do this and it brought Kathryn peace-of-mind to have a symbol of Harry's legacy.

Weeks later, Kathryn called me in a panic. Her desperation nearly broke my heart. She was really upset with herself. "I can't remember what Harry wanted on his memorial."

I could feel Harry at that moment saying, "you know."

I felt so privileged to have this information to share. "It's the quote from the Parisian *Magazine Litteraire*."

She laughed and knew exactly what he wanted.

It was shortened for his headstone, but the original quote is as follows:

"For the past 25 years, we in France have considered Whittington one of the masters of the *roman noir* in the second generation-after Hammett, Chandler, Cain of the first generation… his BRUTE IN BRASS is one of the finest of the genre ever written…"

The weeks and months that followed Harry's death were emotional. Kathryn and I got together at their home and reminisced.

Harry shared at one point, that all he wanted to do at the end of his life was write a book and die. Go to sleep. He did that for the most part.

The Hawaiian novel was never published. However, I wrote the novel "Marquel" (that he approved) in 53 days not long after he passed. I wrote a chapter a day as he did.

I didn't publish "Marquel" right away but focused on family. I didn't have Harry's courage to quit working and write.

I named the book after our daughter Marquel. Which was a goal I had set for myself as a 15-year-old, to write a novel and have a daughter with the same name.

Within a year of Harry's passing, our daughter Blair was born and the next novel popped into my head. It washed around in my thoughts for years as my husband and I focused on raising our family.

As time went by, I got busy again. My calls to Kathryn eventually became annual Christmas cards. We got together when Harry's western novels were donated to the University of Wyoming. Kathryn was so pleased that a part of Harry's work would have a permanent place of honor. I knew she wanted his whole library to have a home. Our time together was always about remembering Harry. She has since joined him in heaven.

As our daughters grew and moved on to film and acting careers, they made a book-trailer for my novel, "Marquel" in 2013 starring our daughter, Marquel and actor Eric Roberts.

I wrote the next book and published it. It is named for Blair, our filmmaker daughter and it's titled, "St. Blair: Children of the Night."

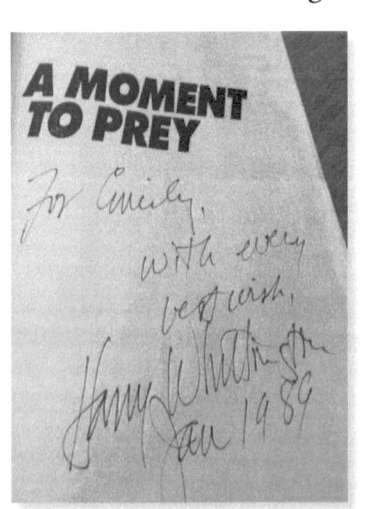

I have shared with our girls that with Harry's encouragement, I became a novelist and now with their encouragement, I am reigniting my dream.

But I will never forget Harry and the gift he gave me in sharing his talent, his heart and his final wishes. I am honored to re-introduce him to a new generation in this short memoir.

Thank you, Harry!

Harry and Kathryn Whittington's final resting place. Harry's legacy is set in stone.

Kathryn sent this picture with a note after the funeral.

F is for Fiction

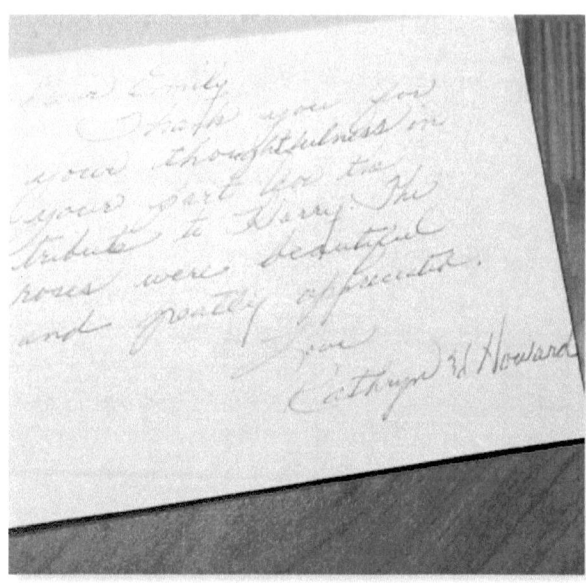

A note from Kathryn.

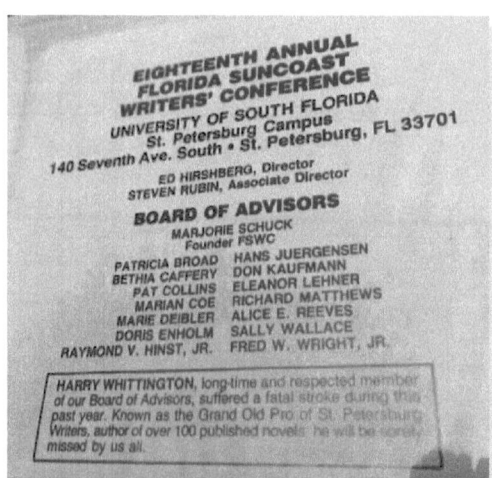

FL Suncoast Writers' Conference brochure
the year Harry passed.

Harry's director's chair.
All Photos by Emily W. Skinner

Sun and Sand—Friday – September 10, 1982

Tucked Away In Indian Rocks ... A Writer With Many Names

By Emily L. Williams

Florida is known for its sunshine, tourists, and oranges. But one thing maybe we don't think of too often is its writers. Our state has been graced with the names Ernest Hemingway, Tennessee Williams, John D. MacDonald and one that many of you may be unaware of...Harry Whittington.

Whittington, a resident of Indian Rocks Beach, has written 110 novels and has no desire to ever quit the writing profession. "I'm never going to retire," the 67-year-old writer says, "I think the perfect way to go (die) would be to finish a book, go to bed and just never wake up."

He began his long and successful writing career at the age of 16. At that time he tried his hand, as many have, at writing short stories. However, it wasn't until seven years later, in 1943, that he sold his first short story to the Chicago Times for $15.

"That was the proudest $15 I ever made," Whittington says. And you'd probably assume that he wrote like crazy to sell many more short stories afterward, but Harry decided to hold off. Later drafted into the Navy, Whittington began to take G.I. writing courses while serving his country.

"It was then that the scales fell out from under me," Whittington says. "It's like a light came on--so that's how you do it (writing)," Whittington explains.

Harry Whittington with a gesture, throwing his arms in the air. "I'd been writing stories and one would turn out good and another wouldn't--after the course I realized that there was a reason—a method."

"It's the complication idea. Meaning, what you write about is how to solve a problem. I didn't realize it until then and after I wrote like mad," Whittington says.

In 1945 Whittington sold his first novel, *Vengeance Valley* and made $500 from the sale.

Whittington's Indian Rocks home exudes his success. His office, a bedroom conversion, overlooks the bay. The walls around him are shelved with books, those which he has written and others as well.

In the center of the room is his writing domain. Almost completely surrounded by desks, Whittington works six hours-a-day, five days-a-week at his craft.

However, he can remember a time when his two children were young--there was no office or desk to work from.

"I used to lay everything out on the bed and pull up a small table and put my typewriter on it and sit on the bed, while the children used to run around the room playing.

"Nothing bothered me then, the children could make their noise and I'd work and never notice them. Now, if anyone disturbs me, well that's it," Whittington says.

"This is a business to me. You know when I started out l didn't know that you weren't supposed to make a living at freelancing. I was too dumb to know that," Whittington says. And where has that gotten him? In October, Harry Whittington and his wife

Kathryn will travel to Reims, France where Harry will be the guest of honor at the professional and amateur writers', Detective Story and Movie Festival.

Jean- Jacques Schleret of Paris writes of Whittington's works

"... for the past 25 years, we in France have considered Whittington one of the masters of the roman-noir in the second generation–after Hammett, Chandler, Cain, of the first generation… his novel *Hell Can Wait* is one of the finest of the genre ever written…"

Whittington 's following in Europe is as vast as the novels he has written. For those of you who are wondering why, perhaps, you haven't seen a book on your local bookstore shelf by Harry Whittington, maybe it is because you're looking for the wrong name.

"When I first started out, I wrote everything by Harry Whittington. Then I discovered that people look for you under a certain category. If they saw Harry Whittington under a western novel, they wouldn't look for you under a historical. So I started using different names for different types of books," Whittington explains.

If you're now wondering what or (who) to look for, Whittington's books can be found under the names, Whit Harrison, Hallam Whitney, Harriett Kathryn Myers, Kel Holland, Clay Stuart, Howard Winslow, Henri Whittier, Blaine Stevens, and Ashley Carter.

In 1979 Whittington received both the Silver Porgy Award for *Panama*, by Ashley Carter as the best paperback novel based on fact and the Bronze Porgy Award for *Rampage* by Harry Whittington as the best contemporary paperback novel.

His book, *Taproot of Falconhurst* made number 29 on the paperback bestseller list in its first week. However, *The Doomsday Affair* one of the "Man From Uncle" series number two, spent a year on the paperback bestseller list, ironic to Whittington since he felt his other novels might be more worthy of the honor.

"I was only paid $1,500 to write that one and look at where it went—it just shows you that you never know. I still get letters from little kids saying how much they enjoyed that book," Whittington says.

The 42nd edition of *Who's Who in America* 1982-83, Volume 2, lists the Indian Rocks Beach author as saying, "I tell my seminar audiences a truth they sooner or later learn is basic: I wrote what I wanted to write and for seven years sold nothing. Then I began to write what editors wanted, and I sold everything wrote--as fast as could write it!"

In 1957, Whittington was bitten by the movie bug and moved to Burbank, California and became a screenwriter for Warner Brothers Studio. But this didn't last long. When he returned to Florida, he decided to make a movie of own.

"I really had the bug and this was a time when the horror movies were really big. So I wrote, produced and directed "Face of the Phantom." It cost a fortune to make and it was never shown," Whittington says.

Though Whittington says he never quit writing, he did attempt to quit once between 1968-1975. It was shortly after the "Man From Uncle" book came out. "After that book and the way it went (sold) I thought I was washed up," he says. Whittington was not pleased that it was that particular book that became so popular.

"So, I decided to quit writing books and I moved to Washington, D.C. and became a writer for the government, writing speeches and editing different papers," he says.

However, it is obvious that he dearly loves his craft. When talking about techniques, character developments, titles, plots, or anything that has to do with writing, his face lights up and smiles, and he then relaxingly sits back reveals his style.

"I believe in total preparation—a full and complete plot. I know some say that today there is a free style--but I want to know where that story is going.

"I first outline my book and then outline my chapters. Sometimes in my chapter outline just one word will keep an idea for me," Whittington says.

Pulling a yellow sheet of legal paper from the trash can, he shows just how he's prepared a chapter for his latest book *Dark Ran the River*. The crumbled paper contained action sentences that mapped out just what his characters were doing. And in place of a sentence here and there, one word as he explained was key, for a particular point in the chapter.

Whittington also believes that titles are important to a book. However, he says that his literary agent, Liz Trupin, believes just the opposite.

"We disagree here and there, but I do sincerely believe that a title is important.

Look at Dicken's *A Tale of Two Cities*, why the title is perfect and it just puts the story together.

"I like to make up titles—sometimes you can get an idea for a book that way. Often I start with the title and develop my story from there.

"I almost ruined a luncheon with Louis L'Amour (a well-known western writer) by saying that. He believes that your title has to come from somewhere in the book," Whittington says.

Of the varying types of books that he has written, Whittington's favorites are the historical. It takes him roughly 3 months to write a historical novel and he tries to write at least two a year.

Looking back to 1951, a record year for Harry Whittington, he wrote 15. They bought novels. "They bought fast, so I wrote fast," he says. Since then, however, he averages about six books a year.

An admirer of F. Scott Fitzgerald, Whittington tells anyone who wants to be a writer, "You have to start yesterday and read the books that are selling. And if you follow the guidelines of one of those, you should have no trouble selling your own," he says.

Reflecting on his long and successful career—doing as so many wish they could do—something that makes them happy, Whittington says, "I've been the luckiest person to ever live."

tion idea. Meaning, what you write about is how to solve a problem. I didn't realize it until then and after that I wrote like mad," Whittington says.

In 1945 Whittington sold his first novel, Vengeance Valley and made $500 from the sale.

Whittington's Indian Rocks home exudes his success. His office, a bedroom conversion, overlooks the bay. The walls around him are shelved with books, those which he has written and others as well.

In the center of the room is his writing domain. Almost completely surrounded by desks, Whittington works six hours-a-day, five days-a-week at his craft. However, he can remember a time when his two children were young--there was no office or desk to work from.

"I used to lay everything out on the bed and pull up a small table and put my typewriter on it and sit on the bed, while the children used to run around the room playing.

"Nothing bothered me then, the children could make their noise and I'd work and never notice them. Now, if anyone disturbs me, well that's it," Whittington says.

"This is a business to me. You know when I started out I didn't know that you weren't supposed to make a living at freelancing. I was too dumb to know that," Whittington says. And where has that gotten him? In October, Harry Whittington and his wife Kathryn will travel to Reims, France, where Harry will be the guest of honor at the professional and amateur writers', Detective Story and Movie Festival.

Jean-Jacques Schieret of Paris writes of Whittington's works "... for the past 25 years, we in France have considered Whittington one of the masters of the roman-noir in the second generation--after Hammett, Chandler, Cain, of the first generation ... his novel Hell Can Wait is one of the finest of the genre ever written..."

Whittington's following in Europe is as vast as the novels he has written. For those of you who are wondering why, perhaps, you haven't seen a book on your local bookstore shelf by Harry Whittington, maybe it is because you're looking for the wrong name.

"When I first started out, I wrote everything by Harry Whittington. Then I discovered that people look for you under a certain category. If they saw Harry Whittington under a western novel, they wouldn't look for you under a historical. So I started using different names for different types of books," Whittington explains.

If you're now wondering what or (who) to look for, Whittington's books can be found under the names, Whit Harrison, Hallam Whitney, Harriett Kathryn Myers, Kel Holland, Clay Stuart, Howard Winslow, Henri Whittier, Blaine Stevens, and Ashley Carter.

In 1979 Whittington received both the Silver Porgy Award for Panama, by Ashley Carter as the best paperback novel based on fact and the Bronze Porgy Award for Rampage by Harry Whittington as the best comtemporary paper back novel.

His book, Taproot of Falconhurst made number 29 on the paperback bestseller list in its first week. However, The Doomsday Affair one of the "Man From Uncle" series number two, spent a year on the paperback bestseller list, ironic to Whittington since he felt his other novels might be more worthy of the honor.

"I was only paid $1,500 to write that one and look at where it went--it just shows you that you never know. I still get letters from little kids saying how much they enjoyed that book," Whittington says.

The 42nd edition of Who's Who in America 1982-83, Volume 2, lists the Indian Rocks Beach author as saying, "I tell my seminar audiences a truth they sooner or later learn is basic: I wrote what I wanted to write and for seven years sold nothing. Then I began to write what editors wanted, and I sold everything I wrote-as fast as I could write it!"

In 1957, Whittington was bitten by the movie bug and moved to Burbank, California and became a screenwriter for Warner Brothers Studio. But this didn't last long. When he returned to Florida he decided to make a movie of his own.

"I really had the bug and this was a time when the horror movies were really big. So I wrote, produced and directed "Face of the Phantom." It cost a fortune to make and it was never shown," Whittington says.

Though Whittington says he'll never quit writing, he did attempt to quit once between 1968-75. It was shortly after the "Man From Uncle" book came out.

"After that book and the way it went (sold) I thought I was washed up," he says. Whittington was not pleased that it was that particular book that became so popular.

"So I decided to quit writing books and I moved to Washington D.C. and became a writer for the government, writing speeches and editing different papers," he says.

However, it is obvious that he dearly loves his craft. When talking about technicques, character developments, titles, plots, or anything that has to do with writing, his face lights up and smiles, and he then relaxingly sits back and reveals his style.

"I believe in total preparation--a full and complete plot. I know some say that today there is a free style--but I want to know where that story is going.

"I first outline my book and then I outline my chapters. Sometimes in my chapter outline just one word will keep an idea for me," Whittington says.

Pulling a yellow sheet of legal paper from the trash can, he shows just how he's prepared a chapter for his latest book Dark Ran the River. The crumbled paper contained action sentences that mapped out just what his characters were doing. And in place of a sentence here and there, one word as he explained was his key, for a particular point in the chapter. Whittington also believes that titles are important to a book. However, he says that his literary agent, Liz Trupin,

See WRITER, page 8

Photos of articles by Emily W. Skinner

Tucked Away In Indian Rocks ...
A Writer With Many Names

By Emily L. Williams

Florida is known for its sunshine, tourists, and oranges. But one thing maybe we don't think of too often is its writers. Our state has been graced with the names Ernest Hemingway, Tennessee Williams, John D. MacDonald and one that many of you may be unaware of ... Harry Whittington.

Whittington, a resident of Indian Rocks Beach, has written 110 novels and has no desire to ever quit the writing profession. "I'm never going to retire," the 67-year-old writer says, "I think the perfect way to go (die) would be to finish a book, go to bed and just never wake up."

He began his long and successful writing career at the age of 16. At that time he tried his hand, as many have, at writing short stories. However, it wasn't until seven years later, in 1943, that he sold his first short story to the Chicago Times for $15.

"That was the proudest $15 I ever made," Whittington says. And you'd probably assume that he wrote like crazy to sell many more short stories afterward, but Harry decided to hold off. Later drafted into the Navy, Whittington began to take G.I. writing courses while serving his country.

"It was then that the scales fell out from under me," Whittington says. "It's like a light came on--so that's how you do it (writing)," Whittington explains with a gesture, throwing his arms in the air.

"I'd been writing stories and one would turn out good and another wouldn't--after the course I realized that there was a reason--a method."

"It's the complica-

"I'm never going to retire. I think the perfect way to go (die) would be to finish a book, go to bed, and just never wake up."
--Harry Whittington

J.J.Schleret for Les Amis Du Crime No. 5, and translated by Jean-Francois Naudon
March 1980 edition devoted to Harry Whittington
Photo of brochure by Emily W. Skinner

Plotting like Harry

One question I get asked and I'm never quite clear what writers are expecting—but many want to hear how Harry wrote *the way* he did, referring to his voice and style. If you can imagine quitting a good job with benefits (he was a mailman) and suddenly becoming a trapeze artist without a net, you might understand how he cultivated his fast, often self-deprecating dialogue that cut to the point. It's worth repeating that in his *I Remember It Well* foreword of a 1987 Black Lizard release, Harry said, "The reason why I wrote and sold more than almost everyone else was that I was living on the edge of ruin, and I was naïve."

Thus, his pulp novels are swift because publishers were buying as quickly as he could finish. You feel the tension. To accomplish this, he fully outlined his novels and followed the outline exactly. He also wrote in finished mode. He would go back through his stories and tweak, and I'm sure with his historical novels there were more rewrites, but those earlier short stories and hard-boiled novellas were written in a completed style that didn't permit him much downtime. Nor did he want downtime. From my perspective, he wrote like a man without time. Like a death row inmate awaiting clemency from a governor just moments before being strapped to the electric chair. Do you feel the urgency? If so, you'll get his voice.

French publication, *Les Amis Du Crime No. 5*, 1980, translated by Jean-Francois Naudon from comments collected by J.J. Schleret September 1978 to October 1979, from an English questionnaire Harry answered and was translated to French, which I translated back to English, Harry said his novel theme, "is that of the alone man placed in unusual situations." When asked how he would describe his hero, Harry said, "For me, he is the last of the knights. A brave man who knows that his cause and his armor are rusty; who knows that the Duke for whom he fights is a real bastard, and that it is against the Duke, not against the Dragon, that he will turn his blunt sword. I believe he remains optimistic in the face of disaster. He believes in himself when he is forced to doubt everything else. I try to love him and I hope that the reader will, with me, want to see him triumph over the impossible situations in which he finds himself."

This guide is based on my understanding of his process from my initial interview as well as working directly with him on his last novel.

1. Once you have your title or general idea, decide if it falls into a specific genre.
   Genre examples: Science Fiction, Mystery (Mysteries have subgenres, like cozy mystery, medical mystery, etc.), Western, Romance (Romance novels vary, too. Historical, erotica, adult contemporary, etc.). Google genres.
2. If your genre is trending, look to see what books are currently selling in that genre and who the top authors are. Look at Amazon's, *New York Times*,' and *USA Today*'s bestseller list.
3. Read the synopsis of the bestsellers. This will also help you structure your synopsis and prepare to build your story.

4. Read at least three bestsellers in your genre.
5. While you are reading these books, take notes on each chapter. What happened? How were the characters presented? What drives these characters? How are they described? Each author has a unique voice and style. You will find your unique voice and style once you start writing. Don't get bogged down with another author's phrases or sentences but instead understand whether their writing is descriptive or short to the point. Pacing is important. Some novels are a slow burn others end each chapter on a cliffhanger to keep you turning the pages. Pace yours similar to the bestsellers in your genre.
6. What does the bestseller's main character want? What does your main character want? It's helpful to start aligning the notes you've taken with the ideas you have for your book. Do a side-by-side comparison on a notepad.
7. What holds the main character back? Why does this trait or circumstance hold the main character back? Is the obstacle insurmountable? Or perceived to be insurmountable? How does the lead overcome the hurdle and get what they want? Or lose what they have?
8. Harry believed in plausibility. Having a main character wake from a bad dream to solve an impossible problem might work for a handful of stories, but readers want realistic plot lines and climaxes. They also want to join the characters on the journey. Show versus tell. A reader should be able to go back through the story and find the clues they missed and come to the same conclusion as the final chapter. If not, the reader may feel they've wasted their time.
9. Twists in the story have to be set up. Some novels twist and twist and twist without giving the reader any clues.

This goes to point #8. If the twist is a unique circumstance, health issue or disaster to avert, do your research. Write your character's backstory and refer to it as needed. Example, does the lead have a deadly peanut allergy? How does the hero save a victim being held hostage in a peanut butter manufacturer's warehouse?

10. Your key, as Harry called it, should be seeded in the beginning of your story and nourished throughout the distractions your secondary characters and events place in the protagonist's way. In *Romeo and Juliet* Harry is quoted as saying in a *Writer's Digest* article, November 1972, *Plotting the Short Story*, "The basic key he (Shakespeare) came up with was: A certain potion causes a catalytic trance resembling death. This is the key that resolved R&J." Working from the key, an author has an inside track to building the story.

11. Outline your entire book, including how many pages you expect each chapter to be. Go back to the bestsellers in the genre you will be competing with. How many pages are there? Is there a tempo?

    <u>Harry shared in our interview</u>: "I believe in total preparation—a full and complete plot. I know some say that today there is a free style—but I want to know where that story is going. I first outline my book and then outline my chapters. Sometimes in my chapter outline just one word will keep an idea for me."

12. Follow your outline. I wrote my novel *Marquel* in 52 days following a complete outline. But sometimes your characters will take you down a road that doesn't follow the outline. That happened to me when writing the sequel to *Marquel*. I wrote a full outline for *Marquel's Dilemma*. As

soon as I started writing, the characters went off track, so much so, I just kept writing expecting to jump in at some point and redirect them to the outline. Instead, the sequel outline became book three's outline for *Marquel's Redemption*. This defied what Harry taught me, but it didn't. My characters had a story that took me to my outline, I just didn't know I was missing a lot of drama my characters experienced. That's the fun part of writing. You develop relationships with your characters and they become your friends. They tell you, their story. I wrote the second book in twenty days. Once finished, I had my outline ready for book three and it took thirty days to write.

13. An outline gives you the freedom to write chapters out of sequence. You could write your last chapter first. I've done this. Not that Harry did it this way, but his method provides that option. If you get stuck, try it. It's liberating to not force yourself into writing an action you might not be ready to tackle on a given day. Since you will be rewriting, you can fix any bumps in continuity on the rewrite. Just follow the outline.

14. Write a chapter a day. The outline tells you how many pages. Harry wrote six to eight hours a day and enjoyed the satisfaction of completing at least one chapter a day. He might write two. Stick to this practice and you'll find yourself completing projects in record time.

15. Write to sell. Harry studied the markets and wrote in multiple genres because he was a working author. By treating his craft as a business, he painstakingly earned a living as a traditionally published author.

Photos of articles by Emily W. Skinner

In Conclusion

Wow, I *was* a working writer, having saved this evidence. The biggest surprise was recalling the wide variety of stories I covered. Here you'll find Melissa Manchester's press releases, my questions, my typed copy, and the generous spread printed in *The Clearwater Sun*. The Emlyn Williams interview was my least favorite, as mentioned earlier. The photo of Leon Everette and me shows my tape recorder and note pad. I really like these photos. Ronnie McDowell ran out of his bus for a brief photo before the band drove off. Everette and McDowell both performed at the Orange Blossom Jamboree. That was my first time backstage for an entire event and I drank too much beer in the press tent. Not that anything happened, other than my running up to McDowell's bus in the mud and banging on the door for a photo. Live and learn. In time I would eventually call the *Rolling Stone* to pitch a local band whereby they told me to send the story in. Seriously! On spec, of course. I want to believe I talked to Jann Wenner or Ben Fong-Torres, but I really don't know who I spoke with. I still haven't found those notes. The band I interviewed performed a gig in Britain and had a song trending overseas. Okay, at some point, I did date their drummer. But when I showed up for the interview, the lead singer, Tom Gribbin, told me he was expecting a reporter from the *Rolling Stone*. I was so excited for them! Then I realized

I was the interviewer for *Rolling Stone*. Then I felt bad for them. I was working on a freelance piece I pitched to *Rolling Stone*. He was fine, but my confidence dropped dramatically. If I didn't sell the article (which I didn't), I would feel I had wasted their time. I did publish a local story about the band, but I felt like a fraud. I wasn't a fraud. I was truly trying to break into national magazines and apparently my pitching skills were better than my writing.

The plastic surgery magazine article below was an especially memorable interview whereby I felt like I wanted to pass out from the doctor's graphic descriptions. I eventually stretched out on his couch to avoid keeling over. Yep! I am very good at visualization. But embarrassment got the better of me and I popped right back into writer mode and got the job done. Dr. Coates said I recovered faster than most people do when experiencing vasovagal syncope, a sudden drop in heart rate or blood pressure triggered by emotions, often happens at the sight of blood. And as I wrap up this book, I learned in *The Freaks Came Out to Write* by Tricia Romano that the *Village Voice* sought amateurs to write for their paper! Norman Mailer (co-founder) and staff wanted the village (New York City) stories without restricting the villagers' voice. OMG! Several of their amateurs and rogue reporters wrote without punctuation or some in capitalization at times, Romano wrote. A hodge podge of styles. I mean seriously! I beat myself up this entire memoir only to learn that I could've been a freak! Geez! But in hindsight, I also realized my *Bohemian Chronicle* had *Voice* aims.

But destiny determined that I needed an income and professional exposure outside of writing, especially for my family's future. The income was more than I would have believed was possible from youth. The professional skills acquired have benefited me in numerous ways to the irritation of some of my bosses in that I have become a sometimes-relentless questioner of processes. The universe recognized I could sell. My determination and organizational skills made the work enjoyable. I often saw my coworkers and clients as characters. I would be in a meeting and hear something funny that took me out of the meeting to develop a story in my thoughts about the individuals in the room. It kept me sane. Having built my technique pitching articles to editors, I discovered in this memoir that I had been selling all along. And now I have happily returned to writing in retirement. I do have a couple of screenplays in the works, but beyond that, I'm still thinking. Thank you for reading.

Me, my tape recorder and notepad with Leon Everette.

Emily and Ronnie McDowell. I think McDowell wanted to strangle me for stopping the bus.

Photos taken by a Steppin Out photographer and unfortunately not labeled.

F is for Fiction

Photos of articles by Emily W. Skinner

Sun Spectrum
E
Anclote Manor: one man's dream
Hospital founder
DIAZ AND MEDINA

HEALTH/MEDICAL
The Look of Success:
NEWSLETTER
Suction-Assisted
Lipectomy
Reducing Body
Fat

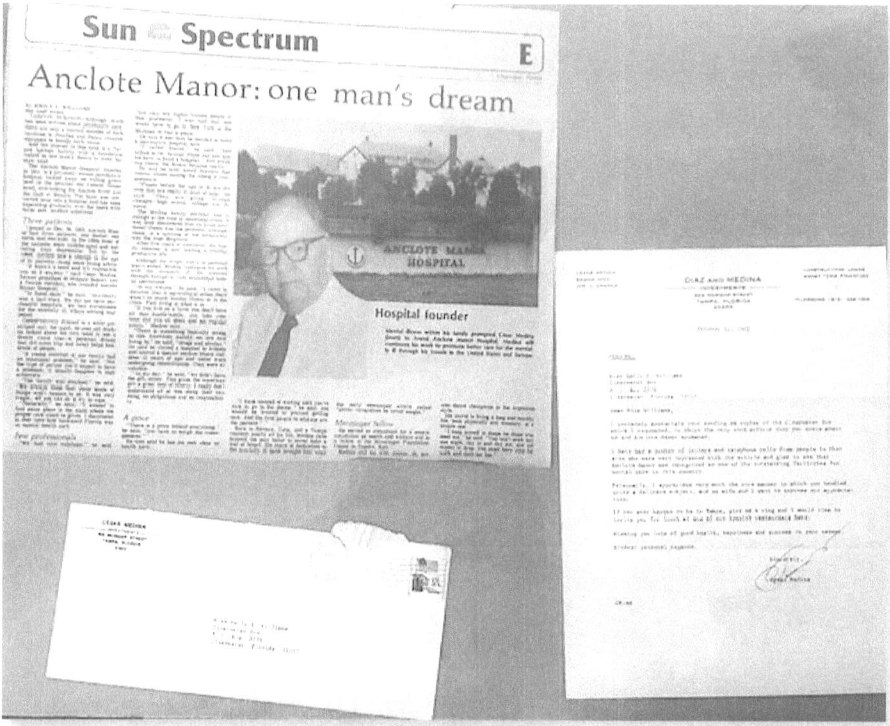

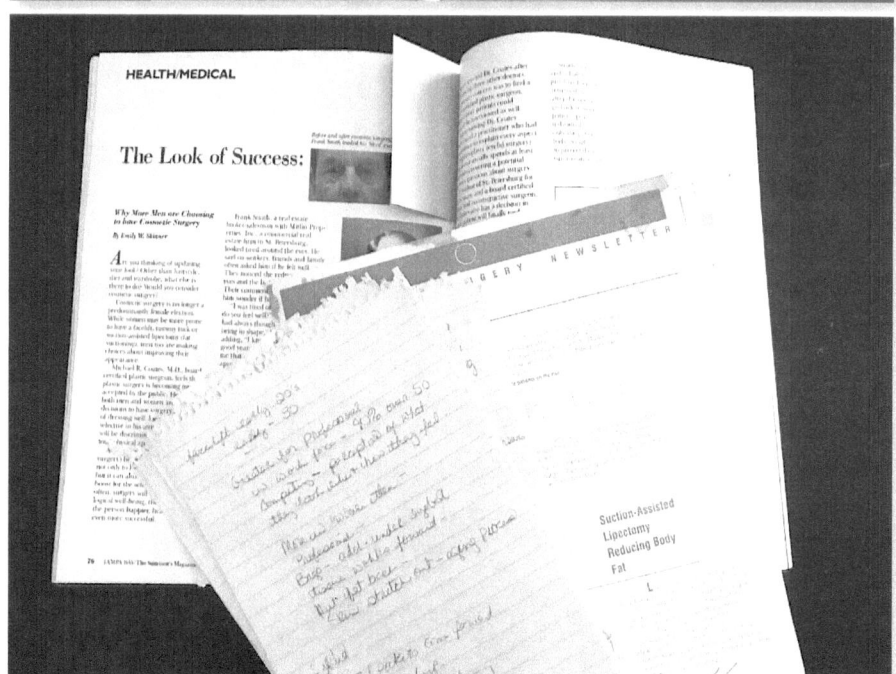

F is for Fiction

Photos of articles by Emily W. Skinner

Tom Gribbin...
Local Musician Returns Home After Successful Gigs In Britain

Creators serious about Comedy Magazine

Sex farce
Noel Harrison plays director in a play within a play

By EMILY W. SKINNER

Noel Harrison, star of the national touring company of "Noises Off," originally sought his career in film direction.

In "Noises Off," Harrison plays the director of a two-bit sex farce, "Nothing On."

"Noises Off," which means commotion in the wings, presents a seedy British acting troupe touring small towns of England who have their own behind-the-scenes sex farce. In the play, actors play actors in a play within a play. Sound confusing? Reading the play sometimes is, but nevertheless hilarious. Harrison explained that performing in the show itself is not confusing, yet what the audience sees on stage appears so.

"Learning the part and the actual mechanics of the second act is what is challenging," Harrison said in a phone interview from Virginia, where the show played recently. "If this were chaotic in the minds of the actors, this could be disastrous."

"Noises Off" was conceived by British satirist Michael Frayn as he stood in the wings watching a performance of a quick-change comic farce he had written for Lynn Redgrave and Richard Briers. Frayn thought that what was going on backstage was funnier that what was on stage.

The result? "Noises Off."

Harrison said he feels all actors experience a certain deja vu when they see "Noises Off."

"We've all gone through some of these experiences," the 51-year-old actor said. "I respond in one scene the same way a director in a show I was in re-

NOEL HARRISON
... 'Noises Off'

sponded. You can use some experiences in the part."

Harrison is a diversified entertainer. The son of "My Fair Lady" 's leading man Rex Harrison, Noel has received recognition as an actor, singer, musician, composer, director, craftsman, builder and world class skier.

Harrison sang "Windmills of Your Mind" on the soundtrack of the film "The Thomas Crown Affair," as well as singing at various club engagements. He has had two Top 40 hits, "A Young Girl" by Charles Aznavour, and "Suzanne." He was also a member of the British Olympic Ski Team in 1952 and 1956 and placed first in the British Ski Championships. His acting credits include BBC television films and the television show "The Girl from

U.N.C.L.E.," in which he co-starred with Stephanie Powers.

Harrison — father of three children, Cathryn, Simon and Harriet, by his first wife Sara Tufnell and twins Chloe and William by second wife Margaret — also has played the role of Professor Henry Higgins (made famous by his father) in the Lerner and Loewe musical "My Fair Lady" nine times.

"If I live long enough I hope to direct this son) Simon in a 50th anniversary production of 'My Fair Lady,' in 2006. He (Simon) should be just the right age about then," Harrison said.

When asked what trait or characteristic, good or bad, he feels that he may have inherited from his father, he responded: "That's a different way of putting it. I don't think we're much alike. We had lunch the day before yesterday. And I guess I would say his voice. When I'm at his house and I answer the phone most people think I'm him."

After the current tour of "Noises Off" ends, Harrison will head to Texas to play King Arthur in "Camelot" and he will also appear in a production of "South Pacific."

Though Harrison considers directing the passion of his life, he seems most content playing the director of "Nothing On" in "Noises Off."

"Noises Off" will be presented today and Friday, Jan. 23-24, at 8 p.m. at Ruth Eckerd Hall, 1111 McMullen-Booth Road. Tickets are $24.95, $20.95, $17.95 and $16.95 and are available at the box office or by phoning 725-1844.

Vol. IX No. 19   January 7, 1988

Commission starts new year on positive note

by Emily W Skinner

F IS FOR FICTION

Photos of articles by Emily W. Skinner

Live-aboard boat owners may have to cruise to new quarters

by Emily W. Skinner

"Live-aboard" boat owners in Clearwater may have to obtain a their holding tanks three miles offshore, according to coast guard regulations. However, Held said,

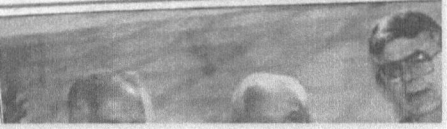

Sunset Sam awaits a mate

by Emily W. Skinner

Will Sunset Sam have a mate or a buddy? The saga continues.

According to Dennis Kellenberger, Clearwater Marine Science Center director, the mating part will be up to a lady dolphin named Fathom. That is, if she even makes it to the center.

Kellenberger is quite confident that Fathom will indeed arrive, however, he notes the final paper work has not yet been approved. Fathom is currently residing at the Oklahoma City Zoo where she performed in an attraction "from a feeding standpoint," Kellenberger said.

It wasn't until the zoo officials began preparing Fathom for the move to Clearwater they

problems," Kellenberger said. "Originally . . . they were treating her for pneumonia.

However, Kellenberger explained that since Fathom had responded to the zoo's original treatment for pneumonia they (the zoo) probably never X-rayed the dolphin until recently.

"You don't X-ray every animal you treat," Kellenberger said.

Fathom is being donated by the Oklahoma City Zoo to the Clearwater Marine Science Center. It was Kellenberger's original hope that Fathom would be a mate for Sunset Sam, a handicapped dolphin whose permanent home is the center.

Whether Fathom mates with Sam is no longer a concern,

Winners honored on I.E. for a fantasy island

Harris' last stab at 'Camelot' disappoints

By EMILY W. SKINNER
Sun correspondent

"Camelot," the first of this season's Broadway in the Sunshine productions, missed the mark opening night.

If dependent only on costuming and sets, this show could have been a success. But technical difficulties and a lethargic performance by Richard Harris made for a disappointing evening at Tuesday's press opening.

Perhaps Harris who also directed the show, was too preoccupied with the bugs in the sound system and the awkward exits of some performers. However, this does not account for the poor vocal range of the 51-year-old actor. One woman turned to her husband and said, "I liked him when he was talking, but his singing

For those who remember the motion

Review

picture "Camelot," in which Harris starred, this production would seem campy and superficial by comparison. Harris' young Arthur in Act I Scene 1 is lifeless and boring. The show really doesn't pick up until Scene 6, and even then it is like riding a roller coaster. This is particularly so in Act II.

Just when the audience begins to feel a little emotion, a rush of speeches, songs and set changes destroys the mood and makes one care less whether Arthur's heart is breaking or if Guenevere is burned at the stake.

The operatic voices of Martha Traverse, who plays Guenevere, and Gregg Busch, who plays Lancelot, were saving points. But the real scene-stealer was James Val-

entine as King Pellinore.

Valentine played both Merlyn and Pellinore; however, the latter made the show. The bungling old pal of King Arthur's gave every scene a touch of humor and fun, while Busch's Lancelot lacked passion.

What is probably hardest to accept, though, is that Harris just doesn't give Arthur any life. That the actor is obviously older than his character wouldn't matter if the spirit were there. But we never feel Arthur's energy, his soul. And thus, Arthur dies.

On a local television interview, Harris told a reporter that he would not be doing "Camelot" anymore after the current tour ends. Perhaps he feels it is time to lay Arthur to rest.

"Camelot" continues through Sunday at the Bayfront Center, 400 First St. S., St. Petersburg. Call 893-7211.

RICHARD HARRIS
... aging Arthur

Reference Sources in Alpha Order

Acknowledgements
    Cover Designer - https://www.labelschmiede.com/
    Website Designer –https://tomhillmannmediadesign.com

Aaron Sorkin
    Aaron Sorkin – Masterclass.com
    Screenwriting - Masterclass.com

Author Haunts
    Algonquin Round Table https://www.britannica.com/topic/Algonquin-Round-Table
    Andalusia www.atlantamagazine.com/great-reads/asylum-inside-central-state-hospital-worlds-largest-mental-institution/
    Hemingway House - https://www.hemingwayhome.com
    Monroe County Heritage Museum - https://www.tokillamockingbird.com/
    Zora Neale Hurston – zorafestival.org

Bohemian Chronicle
    Zines - https://www.mentalfloss.com/article/88911/brief-history-zines

Book Trailer
    Carson Kressley - https://www.youtube.com/watch?v=1oGNwr-RhjY
    https://www.cameo.com
    Marquel Booktrailer - www.youtube.com/watch?v=6e6O7iYqeVQ

Dough Nuts and More
    Video - Vimeo https://vimeo.com/280220994

F is For Fiction
    W.T. Grants - https://en.wikipedia.org/wiki/W._T._Grant

I Need To Let Harry Go
    Author comparison
    Brewer - https://www.fantasticfiction.com/b/gil-brewer/
    Cain -https://www.fantasticfiction.com/c/paul-cain/
    Caldwell - https://www.southernliterarytrail.org/trail/little-manse-erskine-caldwell-museum
    Chandler - https://www.britannica.com/biography/Raymond-Chandler
    Faulkner - https://en.m.wikipedia.org/wiki/William_Faulkner_bibliography
    Fitzgerald - https://www.biography.com/authors-writers/f-scott-fitzgerald
    Hammett - https://www.britannica.com/biography/Dashiell-Hammett
    Hemingway - https://www.nobelprize.org/prizes/literature/1954/hemingway/bibliography/
    MacDonald - https://www.britannica.com/biography/John-D-MacDonald
    Powell -https://www.fantasticfiction.com/p/talmage-powell/

Steinbeck - https://steinbeck.org/wp-content/uploads/2019/01/Bibliography.pdf
Other
Estate Website - www.harrywhittington.com
Erskine Caldwell - https://www.georgiaencyclopedia.org/articles/arts-culture/erskine-caldwell-1903-1987/
Gainesville Article - https://www.gainesville.com/story/opinion/columns/guest/2015/11/26/joshua-braley-remember-our-regions-bestselling-author/31888333007/
Maxwell Perkins - https://www.britannica.com/biography/Maxwell-Perkins
Plotting article - https://www.writersdigestarchive.com/buy-archive/
Tabor Evans - https://en.wikipedia.org/wiki/Longarm_(book_series)
Webb City - https://www.tampabay.com/news/florida/2019/08/18/webbs-city-closed-40-years-ago-today-what-happened-to-the-worlds-most-unusual-drug-store/
Will Knott - https://www.fantasticfiction.com/k/will-c-knott/

Milton Berle
Friars Club - https://en.wikipedia.org/wiki/Friars_Club_of_Beverly_Hills

Patrick Wayne
IMDB.com - https://www.imdb.com/name/nm0915618/

The Murderer
Coming-of-age - Welldoing.org Jul 10, 2024, by Alice McGurran interviewing Dr Lucy Foulkes. https://

welldoing.org/article/coming-age-life-long-impact-adolescence

William Windom

Skyway Bridge - *https://www.tampabay.com/news/florida/2020/05/08/the-skyway-bridge-collapsed-40-years-ago-heres-how-were-remembering-the-tragedy/*

Photo Sources

I've taken most of these photos from my collection of clips and documents. Anything outside of my personal collection, I provide a source. The Clearwater Sun and its weekly division are no longer in publication. I have also taken all the photos in the Authors Haunts chapter or handed my camera to a family member or bystander to take a photo for my personal album.

Clearwater Sun photo – I found this photo on a generic post on Facebook that had no attribution. I am not able to replicate the search and provide a photo source. It isn't a professional photo and as such, would be considered fair use.

Acknowledgements

A big thank you to former newspaper woman and awesome friend, Gretchen Wells, who has helped me on a few projects. Her editing and proofreading provide me with some much-needed brain rest. To Jim Trupin and Elizabeth Trupin-Pulli of JET Literary Associates, Inc. They were so helpful in putting some of the pieces to the Harry puzzle together. As well a warm hug to Terri Wolf, the Harry Whittington estate's literary agent. To my cover designer Claudia at Labelschmiede.com. We now have seven book covers released, on top of that, she restored my grandmother's photo featured on *Until We Sleep Our Last Sleep*. Consider checking out her website. Special thanks to Tom Hillman at tomhillmannmediadesign.com, who created and manages emilyskinnerbooks.com. And always Lisa DeSpain who is my lifeline for all things publishing. She's formatted all of my books and without her, I don't exist in print or ebook.

To kind friends who continue to read, review, attend booking signings, and encourage me: Carrie Vanerio, Theresa Moser, Susan Brimmer, Beth Swain, Regena Stefanchick, Samantha Alvarez, Jeremiah Cunningham, Catherine Poe, Judi Burten, Kathie Fahey, Muriel Savino, Elaine Duval, CJ and Gregg Fisher, Suzy Rodenbach, Howard (RIP) and Lot Whittington, Ryann Cantrell, Robyn Fairbanks, Susan and Ernie Zager, Judy Roe, Joyce Huslander,

Roxanne Smith, Kim Salter, Marylou Bourdow, Joyce Batdorf, Lynda Lucas, Tracy Brandt, Val Ross, Pam Corkum, Doris Hurst, Jennifer Prange, Peggy Sheffield, Peg Connell (RIP), Kathy Durnell, Laurie Williams, Ramon Mendoza, Pat Lynch, Tampa Theatre Marketing Director, Jill Witecki, and Sheila Ramler. You each provide me motivation to keep in the game. I sincerely appreciate our friendship.

To family members who support me: Tom Skinner, Barbara Williams, John (RIP) and Kathy Williams, Blair Skinner and Caitlin Poley, Marquel and Drew Rogers, Ellen Williams, Cecilia Garrison, John and Robin Williams, Kathleen Sims, Mark Williams, Ruth Skinner, and Selena Sieb. Thanks for the love! Forgive me if I've missed anyone.

Emily Skinner lives in Tampa Bay, Florida with her husband, Tom. In addition to writing, she also enjoys traveling, and working with their daughters, Marquel Skinner and Blair Skinner on their film and acting projects.

Other Books by Emily W. Skinner

Fiction by Emily W. Skinner

Hybrid Medical Thriller/Southern Noir
Mind Hostage

Romantic Suspense
Marquel (Book 1)
Marquel's Dilemma (Book 2)
Marquel's Redemption (Book 3)

Marquel Booktrailer:
Marquel book trailer on YouTube—
featuring actor Eric Roberts & Marquel Skinner
www.youtube.com/watch?v=6e6O7iYqeVQ

Coming of Age Humor
The Movie Queen

Young Adult Novels by E.W. Skinner
St. Blair: Children of the Night (Book 1)
Sybille's Reign (Book 2)
The Diary of St. Blair (Book 3)

Nonfiction by Emily W. Skinner
F Is for Fiction
A nonfiction memoir

Until We Sleep Our Last Sleep:
My Quaker Grandmother's Diary of Faith and
Community Amid Depression and Disability

The Diarist: A companion book for your inspired thoughts

Author events & announcements

www.emilyskinnerbooks.com
www.facebook.com/emilyskinnerbooks
www.instagram.com/emilyauthor

Marquel booktrailer: on YouTube
featuring actor Eric Roberts & Marquel Skinner
www.youtube.com/watch?v=6e6O7iYqeVQ